Teacher Pay
and
Teacher Quality

Dale Ballou
University of Massachusetts at Amherst

Michael Podgursky
University of Missouri—Columbia

1997

W.E.Upjohn Institute for Employment Research
Kalamazoo, Michigan

Library of Congress Cataloging-in-Publication Data

Ballou, Dale.
  Teacher pay and teacher quality / Dale Ballou, Michael Podgursky.
    p. cm.
  Includes bibliographical references (p.) and index.
  ISBN 0–88099–177–1 (alk. paper). — ISBN 0–88099–176–3 (pbk. : alk. paper)
  1. Teachers—Salaries, etc.—United States. 2. Teachers—Recruiting—
United States. 3. Teachers—Supply and demand—United States. 4. Teaching—
Economic aspects—United States.
    I. Podgursky, Michael John. II. Title.
LB2842.22.B35   1997
331.2'81'00973—dc21

96–39941
CIP

Cover design by J. R. Underhill.
Index prepared by Shirley Kessel.
Printed in the United States of America.

Acknowledgments

In the course of this project we have benefited from the advice and comments of many scholars. We are especially thankful to our current and former colleagues Robert Costrell and George Treyz, to Kevin Hollenbeck at the W.E. Upjohn Institute, and to Eric Hanushek, Hamilton Lankford, Tom Downes, Douglas Lambdin, Carolyn Heinrich, Larry Katz, Jim Wilson, Stephen Barro, David Figlio, and seminar participants at Northwestern University, University of Rochester, American Institutes for Research, and the University of Illinois for helpful comments and suggestions. Fred Guy, Lois Yachetta, Sean Campbell and Yan Xing provided valuable research assistance. We are also indebted to Paul Planchon, Dan Kasprzyk, Kerry Gruber, Sharon Bobbit, Tom Smith, Steven Broughman, Peter Stowe, and Alan Morehead at the National Center for Education Statistics, and Beth Schlaline at the National Data Resource Center for technical support and assistance, to Judy Gentry, our editor at the Upjohn Institute, and to two anonymous referees.

We benefited from many hours of interviews with school heads and administrators in various parts of the country. Since these interviews were conducted on the promise of strict confidentiality, we must thank them as a group. We also benefited from discussions with and materials provided by Lynn Cornett and Cheryl Gaines of the Southern Regional Education Board, Dr. Steven Clem of the National Association of Independent Schools, Dr. John Holmes of the Association of Christian Schools International, Dr. Dan Van Der Ark of Christian School International, Dr. Robert Kealey of the National Catholic Education Association, Vincent Durnan of the Northeast Association of Schools and Colleges, Kay James of the Southern Association of Colleges and Schools, Cathy Baird of the North Central Association of Colleges and Schools, Donna Sirutis of the Massachusetts Teachers Association, Chris Yelich of the American Association of Educators in Private Practice, Vickie Glazer of Sylvan Learning Systems Inc., Susan Jacoby and Susan Turner of Berlitz, Jr., Raymond Huntington, President of Huntington Learning Systems, James Boyle of Ombudsman Educational Services, Uda Schultz of SAVIS Educational Systems, Inc., and Inez Bosworth of the Educational Testing Service.

Finally, we are indebted to the W.E. Upjohn Institute for their financial support for this research and, most of all, to our wives and families for their tolerance.

CONTENTS

LIST OF TABLES

LIST OF FIGURES

CHAPTER **1**

Introduction

In 1983, the National Commission on Excellence in Education, a panel of distinguished educators appointed by Secretary of Education Terence Bell, released a report on the condition of American education entitled *A Nation at Risk: The Imperative for Educational Reform*. The provocative message of the report—that if a foreign power had tried to impose on America the mediocre educational performance of our schools, we might well have regarded it as an act of war—set off a debate about the nation's schools that continues today.

Teacher Quality

Not the least of the commission's concerns centered on the quality of teaching. Among their claims were the following:

1. Too many teachers had been poor students themselves.

2. Programs of teacher education placed too much emphasis on courses in educational methods, too little on the subjects to be taught.

3. There were severe shortages of qualified teachers in certain subject areas, such as mathematics and science.

4. Too many newly employed teachers were not qualified to teach the subjects they were assigned.

These concerns were not new. In 1963 the president of the Council for Basic Education described teacher education in the following terms: "A weak faculty operates a weak program that attracts weak students" (Koerner 1963). Researchers reported that SAT scores of education majors ranked near the bottom of all college graduates (Weaver 1983). Subsequent developments confirmed these criticisms, as substantial proportions of the workforce and even larger percentages of new teacher trainees were unable to pass teacher examinations that amounted to little more than tests of basic literacy (Toch 1991).

Worse still, there were signs in the early 1980s that the quality of the teaching workforce was deteriorating. The decline in the average SAT scores of high school seniors intending to major in education had outpaced the drop in scores among college-bound students in general. A similar pattern was found in an analysis of IQ scores of college graduates who entered teaching: in 1967, graduates with IQ scores of 100 and 130 were about equally likely to become teachers; by 1980, the ratio was 4:1 (Murnane et al. 1991).

Problems in teacher recruitment were exacerbated by two other trends. One, women were finding new careers open to them and no longer entered education in the same numbers. This was especially true of bright, capable women who had formerly provided public school systems with a low-cost pool of talented teachers. Second, by the early 1980s, the decline in school enrollments that had marked the previous decade was coming to an end; enrollments began to rise again in the lower elementary grades. Thus policy makers foresaw not only a sustained decline in teacher quality, but an absolute shortage of trained instructors, particularly in critical areas such as mathematics and science (Darling-Hammond 1984).

The Response

By one count, *A Nation at Risk* was followed by more than two hundred reports on American education, each setting out recommendations for educational reform (Wayson 1988). Many proposed to improve teaching effectiveness by raising standards for teacher education and licensing. Such reforms included higher admissions standards for teacher education programs; more rigorous course content in teacher education, with increased emphasis on subject matter; and basic skills and subject matter competency testing for teacher certification. These reforms were, however, unlikely to accomplish much alone. In the words of one of the most prominent studies of the teaching workforce: "It will do little good to raise the standards for entry into the profession of teaching and greatly improve the professional preparation of teachers if nothing is done to make teaching a more attractive career" (Carnegie Forum on Education and the Economy 1986).

The leading reports dealing with teachers were unanimous in regard to one recommendation: in order to attract more capable persons into the profession, salaries needed to be raised (Boyer 1983; The Holmes Group 1986; Carnegie Forum on Education and the Economy 1986; National Commission on Excellence in Education 1983). Over and again it was pointed out that teachers' salaries ranked below those of most occupations requiring a college degree. Moreover, while teaching had never been regarded as a well-paid career, during the 1970s teachers had lost ground. In the ten years that followed the 1971-72 school year, average teacher salaries fell more than 10 percent in constant dollars (U.S. Department of Education 1993). The fact that this decline paralleled a drop in academic ability among new teachers enhanced the case for higher pay.

As state legislatures and local school districts responded to the recommendations of the commissions, a few dissenting voices questioned the accuracy of the diagnosis and efficacy of the cure. It was argued that teachers were not as poorly paid as alleged. Teacher salaries had been understated.[1] In addition, most interoccupational comparisons of salaries omit fringe benefits. Since teachers, like other public sector employees, receive more generous benefits than most private sector workers, this omission led to an understatement of their relative compensation. Finally, teachers also work shorter years than most other Americans; earnings during summer vacations (or the value of leisure) further increase teachers' total income.

More important, there had been no analysis of the teacher labor market to support the recommended salary increases. "[N]o one seems to have any idea of either how much additional teacher talent would be attracted by increases in teacher compensation, or how much students would learn if teachers were paid more" (Lieberman 1986). Indeed, the notion that increasing spending on schools would improve educational outcomes was (and remains) a contentious one, with a substantial body of research failing to detect a strong relationship between per-pupil expenditures and student achievement (Hanushek 1986).

In addition, some doubted that the nation was prepared to spend the sums of money proposed to make teaching competitive with other careers. By one reckoning, the suggestion of the president of the Carnegie Foundation for the Advancement of Teaching to raise teacher salaries by 25 percent after inflation would cost the nation $9 billion annually, not including the cost of additional pension benefits or the increases for others in the education system (such as administrators and clerical staff) that were likely to ensue (Lieberman 1986).

In one respect, at any rate, the skeptics were wrong: the nation proved willing after all to commit vast additional sums to teacher compensation. Although there were large differences across states in the rate of salary growth, on the whole the United States came close to implementing the proposed 25 percent raise. Between 1979 and 1989, teachers' average salaries rose 20 percent after inflation. In some states real increases were extraordinary: 36 percent in New Hampshire, 35 percent in Virginia, 52 percent in Connecticut (U.S. Department of Education 1993).

Increases in salaries for beginning public school teachers substantially restored the competitiveness of teaching vis-a-vis other careers. Between 1979 and 1989, salaries for new teachers rose 13 percent. Average earnings in entry-level positions for all college graduates increased by only 3.5 percent over the same period.[2] By 1991 the ratio of teachers' starting salaries to those of other graduates had reached .86, exceeding the 1976 ratio of 83 percent.

Rather surprisingly, there has been little effort to assess the results of this policy. Surveys conducted by the National Center for Education Statistics now provide more detailed information about the teaching workforce than ever before available, yet no analysis of these data attempting to relate changes in teacher recruitment to salary growth has appeared. Previous scholarly work has focused on pieces of the story (e.g., the relationship between salaries and teacher retention). The analysis of the teacher labor market that would provide the foundation for the formulation of effective policy remains to be done.

In the meantime, the debate over teacher salaries has grown more acrimonious. Voters who have witnessed dramatic increases in teacher compensation without seeing commensurate improvements (at least in their view) in the education provided their children have elected school boards that now pressure teacher unions for salary concessions; teachers are striking because boards have reneged on earlier agreements. Adding to the clamor are the voices of those who believe that teacher salaries are still too low, that we have not done enough to make the profession attractive, and of their opponents who see no point in providing additional funds to an educational system that has demonstrably failed the nation's children and wonder why many of our school systems must now spend upwards of $7,000 per pupil when many private schools cost substantially less.

This monograph is an attempt to clarify the facts as well as the underlying issues in this debate. We ask a simple question: have higher salaries improved the quality of newly recruited teachers? Since we find little evidence to support an affirmative response, we ask two more questions. First, what went wrong?   Second, which reforms are likely to meet with more success? To answer these questions, we review data on the characteristics of newly recruited teachers. We also show how important features of the labor market for teachers systematically undermine efforts to improve teacher quality. Finally, we undertake a comparison of personnel policies and staffing patterns in public and private schools, an exercise that sheds light on what can be accomplished by lifting some of the regulatory (and other) constraints now imposed on public school administrators.

Organization of the Book

The remainder of the text is divided into six chapters. In chapter 2, we take up an important preliminary question—how to measure teacher quality. We select several indicators of quality, which are then used in chapter 3 to assess the evidence on salary growth and teacher recruitment. Chapter 4 offers an analysis of the operation of the teacher labor market that explains our findings, while chapter 5 reviews the implications for teacher recruitment of various other reforms of current interest. Chapter 6 looks at teacher salaries and personnel policies in the private sector to see whether private schools offer a model for reforming public education. Our main points are summarized in the final chapter.

NOTES

1. As Myron Lieberman (1986) points out, *A Nation at Risk* understated the average teacher salary in 1981-82 by 13 percent.

2. Data on real salary growth are from the Surveys of Recent College Graduates, adjusted for changes in the Consumer Price Index. Salary gains by new teachers exceeded those of nonteaching graduates in the humanities (2.6 percent), in the social sciences (5.7 percent), and in science, mathematics, and computer science (11.5 percent).

Various other data are available on salaries of new college graduates. Some of them offer a different picture of the relative wages of teachers. We have used the data that seem to be most broadly representative of the jobs taken by new graduates. An alternative series prepared by the College Placement Council is based on information provided by placement offices. These data are heavily influenced by the results of on-campus recruitment and are not intended to represent the experience of new graduates generally (College Placement Council 1994). Surveys of entry-level salaries at major corporations are even less representative.

Academic studies have also made varying claims about teachers' relative salaries. While there seems to be no dispute that teachers' pay rose in real terms during the 1980s, different claims have been advanced regarding the salaries of teachers relative to college graduates in other occupations. Examining data from the National Longitudinal Survey and the Current Population Surveys, Flyer and Rosen (1996) conclude that relative salaries, while improving during the 1980s, did not recover to the level of the mid-1960s, controlling for teacher education and experience. Hanushek, Rivkin, and Jamison (1992) analyzed data from the Census of Population and concluded that while relative pay improved for male teachers between 1980 and 1990, it fell for women, again conditioning on education and experience.

Some caution is called for when interpreting these numbers. Census and Current Population Survey data provide only rough measures of workforce experience, generally age minus years of education. This is a notoriously poor proxy for the work experience of female teachers, many of whom spend years away from teaching in order to raise families. In addition, while many teachers hold master's degrees, one may reasonably question whether this investment in advanced training is comparable to the additional education represented by other professional degrees.

We do not pursue this question further, since it has no real importance for the thesis of this book. Whether or not teachers' relative pay recovered to earlier levels during the 1980s for the nation as a whole, there is no doubt that salary growth varied considerably across states, both in real and relative terms. It is this variation we examine in chapter 3 to ascertain whether higher pay led to improvements in teacher recruitment.

CHAPTER 2

Indicators of Teacher Quality

This research examines the relationship between teacher salaries and the quality of newly recruited teachers. An important preliminary question is how we intend to measure improvements in the teaching workforce.

Student Achievement

Perhaps the surest sign that schools have been hiring more effective teachers would be improvement in student achievement. Unfortunately, several conceptual and practical difficulties prevent our using such an indicator. (We ignore the question whether standardized tests or some other assessment best measures student learning, since sufficiently many problems arise on other grounds.)

In the first place, it takes time to renew the workforce. Teacher salaries began to rise at the beginning of the 1980s, with the most rapid increase between 1983 and 1986, after the appearance of *A Nation at Risk*. Given the time it takes prospective teachers to react to salary developments and to complete a teacher education program, it is unlikely that much change could have occurred in the quality of new teacher recruits before the middle of the decade. Throughout this period, moreover, new entrants in any given year comprised no more than 5 percent of all teachers. Low rates of entry, coupled with high rates of attrition among new instructors, have kept the share of recently recruited teachers down. Thus in 1991, teachers with no more than three years' experience comprised only 9.7 percent of the workforce (U.S. Department of Education 1993). As a result, it is unlikely that students were exposed to enough newly recruited teachers—even if the latter were, on average, superior to teachers hired earlier—to affect the statistical relationship between teacher salaries and aggregate measures of student performance.

Even if this difficulty could be resolved, any such study faces the problem of distinguishing the impact of new teachers' superior abilities (if such they are) from the fact that inexperience per se reduces their effectiveness. This considerably complicates the investigators' task even when disaggregated data are available, as in the National Educational Longitudinal Study begun in 1988 (NELS-88).

Teacher Attributes

In chapter 1 we reviewed the recommendations of several commissions and task forces concerning teacher recruitment and teacher salaries. Virtually all reports expressed concern about the academic ability of the workforce: the general level of teachers' cognitive skills as well as specific subject-area knowledge. The near-unanimity of these reports suggests that a reasonable assessment of the effect of salary reforms would examine the academic backgrounds of persons newly recruited into teaching. We employ the following indicators:

1. The quality of the college or university that awarded the teacher's bachelor degree, as indicated by the "selectiveness" of the institution, according to Barron's *Profiles of American Colleges*. Ratings are based on entering classes' college board scores and high school records, as well as the percentage of applicants admitted.[1]

2. A degree in an academic subject rather than in education (applicable only to teachers in secondary schools).

3. An undergraduate major in mathematics or science (secondary school teachers only).

4. Undergraduate GPA.

5. SAT scores of prospective education majors.

We do not suppose that these indicators cover all the qualities that contribute to effective teaching or that someone cannot be a good teacher who fares poorly by these measures. Indeed, this much was acknowledged by the task forces and commissions cited above. However, it would seem to be a fair test of salary reform that it improve the workforce where it has been found wanting. In the words of a former assistant secretary of education:

> What I hear from principals is that teachers coming in do not have content background. They have compassion and sensitivity, but they lack the content background to be great teachers (Diane Ravitch, quoted in *The Washington Times*, May 18, 1994).

Even if there were not this consensus among the commissions about the needs of our educational system, a strong case can be made for using these indicators of teacher quality. In the first place, the notion that brighter individuals make better teachers is inherently plausible.

> Teachers should have a good grasp of the ways in which all kinds of physical and social systems work; a feeling for what data are and the uses to which they can be put, an ability to help students see patterns of meaning where others see only confusion. . . . They must be able to learn all the time, as the knowledge required to do their work twists and turns with new challenges and the progress of science and technology. . . . We are describing people of substantial intellectual accomplishment" (Carnegie Forum for Education and the Economy 1986, p. 25)

The research literature also lends support to the proposition that instructors with stronger academic backgrounds are, other things being equal, more effective teachers. Analyzing data on reading achievement of elementary school students in southern California, Winkler (1975) found a positive association between test score gains and the "prestigiousness" of the teacher's undergraduate college. (Prestigious institutions included Stanford and the University of California system; nonprestigious were represented primarily by the California state college system.) In a study of Philadelphia schools, Summers and Wolfe (1977) found that student test score gains between third and sixth grade varied positively with the quality of their teacher's undergraduate college. An analysis of data from *High School and Beyond* found a positive association between student test score gains from tenth to twelfth grades and the selectiveness of the colleges attended by teachers at their school, as rated by Barron's *Profiles* (Ehrenberg and Brewer 1994). The sources of this influence are probably severalfold: the fact that more selective colleges screen applicants on the basis of measures of scholastic aptitude, the higher quality of the education they provide undergraduates (not least of which is a peer effect), and the possibility that these higher achieving students are more enthusiastic about the subjects they teach. Indeed, it has been shown that secondary school teachers who graduated from selective colleges or who majored in the subject they teach assign homework more frequently and put in longer hours grading papers and preparing lessons (Ballou and Podgursky 1995a).

In addition, unless teaching requires a very idiosyncratic set of skills, characteristics that predict success in other fields should help to identify effective teachers as well. Studies of human capital have found a positive relationship between earnings and the quality of the college attended (James et al. 1989; Solmon 1975).[2] College quality also has a positive impact on the likelihood that a new graduate finds a job in the field for which he or she trained (Ballou 1996).

Other research with access to teacher test scores has confirmed the importance of teachers' verbal ability. Several of these studies analyzed data collected by the Office of Equality of Educational Opportunity (OEEO) in the mid-1960s, made famous by the Coleman Report (Coleman et al. 1966): Hanushek (1970); Bowles and Levin (1968); and most recently, Ehrenberg and Brewer (1993). Hanushek (1971) investigated the relationship between the achievement of California third graders and the characteristics of their second and third grade teachers, including experience, hours of graduate education, and scores on a test of verbal ability with more discriminating power than the OEEO exam. Of all teacher characteristics, scores on this exam were the most important determinants of student learning. Webster (1988) found a significant positive correlation between teachers' scores on the Wesman Personnel Classification test, a test of verbal and quantitative ability, and scores of middle school students on the Iowa Tests of Basic Skills as well as the scores of secondary students on the Iowa Tests of Educational Development. Ferguson (1991) reported that student achievement was positively related to district average scores on the Texas Examination of Current Teachers and Administrators (TECAT).

Using data from the Longitudinal Survey of American Youth, Monk (1994) found a strong positive association between the subject matter preparation (college course work) of high school mathematics and science teachers and their students' achievement test scores. The fact that researchers employing a variety of data sets and test instruments have found a positive association between teachers' tested ability and student learning attests to the robustness of this relationship.

It should be noted that not all studies replicate these findings. In particular, some researchers have found that performance on the National Teachers' Examination (NTE) appears to be a poor predictor of teaching ability (Haney et al. 1987). However, Strauss and Sawyer (1986) found that higher NTE scores among North Carolina teachers were inversely related to student failure rates on a standardized competency examination, with a 1 percent increase in teacher quality accompanied by a 5 percent decline in failures. Since the impact of NTE scores on mean student achievement was much weaker, this study reveals the importance of examining more than one outcome measure.

In summary, the link between teachers' cognitive abilities and student learning stands out in a literature that frequently fails to find significant relationships between other teacher attributes and student achievement: "The only reasonably consistent finding seems to be that 'smarter' teachers do better in terms of student achievement." (Hanushek 1981). Moreover, evidence is not limited to scholarly research. An incidental demonstration of the relationship between academic ability and teaching effectiveness occurred during implementation of the Florida master teacher program. Two instruments were used to evaluate teachers: a written test of subject matter knowledge and classroom observation. Participants had to score in the top quartile on both instruments in order to qualify as master teachers. The proportion of successful applicants was one in six (Brandt 1990). Although this figure is sometimes cited as evidence of the low correlation between effective teaching behavior and subject matter knowledge, it demonstrates, of course, precisely the opposite: two-thirds of the teachers who satisfied one criterion also met the other.

Finally, the criteria we propose are currently used by other researchers and policy makers to assess the efficacy of educational reforms. Our choice of indicators is therefore far from idiosyncratic. Changes in SAT scores among prospective education majors have been adduced as evidence that teacher quality is responding to improvements in salary (Kirst and Kelley 1993). The Connecticut State Board of Education cites the percentage of new teachers who graduated from more selective colleges—as rated by Barron's *Profiles*—to demonstrate that higher salaries combined with more rigorous academic standards for new teachers have raised the quality of its teaching workforce (Beaudin, various years). A study of mathematics and science education commissioned by the National Science Foundation recommended that the federal government use the following indicators to monitor the quality of the teaching workforce: undergraduate major, test scores, GPA, and subject area certification (Shavelson et al. 1989). In recent years, states have strengthened requirements in subject area preparation; several now require secondary school teachers to major in the subject they will teach (NASDTEC 1991).

Principals' Ratings of Their Staffs

While we believe that the indicators we have chosen represent reasonable criteria for judging the impact of salary reforms, we are aware that there exist differences of opinion over the importance of these measures. Many educators and researchers deny that there is an important link between what teachers know and how well they teach. The following is a strong but probably fair statement of what many educators believe about the importance of teachers' cognitive ability:

> Given prevailing methods of training and selecting teachers, characteristics such as basic communication skills, general knowledge, professional knowledge, and even knowledge of subject matter taught have small relationship to teaching effectiveness. Whatever the power of such cognitive aspects of teacher qualifications to predict teaching effectiveness, it appears to be no more than that associated with aspects of personality, attitudes, and personal habits (Haney et al. 1987).

This view is not, of course, universal among educators. Indeed, claims that teachers' tested knowledge and academic preparation are unrelated to their ability to teach have been termed preposterous by the president of the National Council for Accreditation of Teacher Education (Wise 1992).

Since opinion is divided, we also include an indicator of teacher quality that is not tied to any particular view of pedagogy but rather reflects the views held by educational practitioners, whatever they may be. The Schools and Staffing Survey of 1990-91 contained an item asking each school principal to rate the quality of his staff. Separate assessments were obtained for new teachers (no more than three years' experience) and experienced staff. This breakdown makes it possible to compare new teachers to experienced teachers, and to measure this change against salary growth. Since the criteria used for these assessments are determined by principals themselves, the relationship between ratings and teacher salaries signals whether principals have been able to recruit staffs that meet their needs, however they conceive them.

Other Indicators

There are two widely used indicators of teacher quality that we do not employ—the percentage of teachers who hold advanced degrees and teachers' experience. Although teacher compensation is generally based on these factors, their demonstrated relationship to teacher quality is slight or nonexistent. Advanced degrees have not been found to improve teacher effectiveness, while the contribution of experience appears weak, at best, and limited to the first few years of teaching (Hanushek 1986). To the extent that higher salaries have raised the proportion of teachers who have taught long enough to become effective, our investigation will understate the consequences of salary reform. (See, however, the discussion of turnover in chapter 4.) Given the overriding importance of recruiting more capable persons into teaching, it seems reasonable to focus on the attributes they bring to their jobs.

To summarize, by the early 1980s, it was widely reported that many of the nation's teachers had weak cognitive skills and poor preparation in their subjects. Such findings prompted recommendations that salaries be raised (along with other measures to improve teacher professionalism). It would seem of considerable interest, then, to learn whether these policies have produced improvements of the kind desired.

NOTES

1. Colleges ranked in the top two categories ("most competitive" and "highly competitive") have been reassigned to a single group ("selective"). At the other end of the scale, colleges rated "less competitive" or "noncompetitive" have also been grouped together ("below average").

2. We use college quality as a broader indicator than do some of the researchers we cite, who ask whether college quality contributes to earnings after one controls for individual ability, family background, etc. The latter question concerns the value added by a college education. By contrast, we use college quality for all that it might represent—as a proxy for higher ability, family inputs, etc., and as a measure of value added during one's undergraduate years. While some of the literature suggests there is little value added from attending a more selective institution, selectivity in the broad sense in which we use it is correlated with subsequent earnings and career opportunities.

CHAPTER 3

Teacher Pay and Recruitment

In this chapter, we investigate the effect that higher salaries have had on the quality of the teaching workforce. This is not the first study to examine the relationship of teacher quality to salaries. Earlier research, exploiting variation in cross-sectional data, has found a modest but statistically significant association between pay and indicators of quality similar to ours. This may indicate that better-paying districts enjoy an advantage in recruitment, though it is also possible that more qualified teachers are drawn to these districts for other reasons (for example, they may be more likely to live in them).[1] While these findings are of interest for some purposes (e.g., assessing effects of disparities in school financing), they primarily reflect the way the market sorts teachers across districts and, as such, say little about the question that concerns us. The commissions and task forces that recommended raising teacher salaries in the early 1980s were not interested in one district's gain at the expense of another, but in the possibility of recruiting into education persons who would otherwise choose more attractive and remunerative careers. Salary coefficients in such studies overstate the increase in teacher quality that results when salaries rise in all schools simultaneously.

This problem does not entirely disappear, of course, at higher levels of aggregation, since high-wage states can recruit teachers away from states with lower levels of pay. However, the evidence on teachers' interstate mobility presented below suggests that using the state as the unit of analysis substantially reduces this bias. And at the national level, no such problem arises. We therefore focus on the relationship between teacher salaries and quality at the state and national levels, beginning with national trends.

National Trends in Teacher Recruitment

We examine data from three sources: SAT scores from the College Board, the Schools and Staffing Surveys (SASS) of 1987-88 and 1990-91, and the Surveys of Recent College Graduates (SRCG), conducted four times between 1981 and 1991. All reported statistics are weighted to take account of stratification and clustering in sample designs. Descriptions of these data sources are provided in appendix 3A.

SAT Scores

We begin with SAT scores of college-bound seniors (College Entrance Examination Board, various years). If recent salary increases have attracted brighter individuals into teaching, evidence to that effect will likely appear in SAT scores of students intending to major in education.[2] Indeed, board scores among prospective education majors have risen. In 1980, combined SAT verbal and math scores among would-be teachers averaged 807, compared to 890 among all examinees. In 1992, the corresponding averages were 850 and 899. Thus over twelve years the gap between prospective education majors and others closed by 50 percent. The number of prospective teachers also rose. In 1980, 6.1 percent of SAT test-takers declared an intention to major in education. By 1992 this proportion had risen to 8 percent.

Quality of College

Figure 3.1 presents information from the 1987-88 SASS on the quality of the institution awarding the teacher's undergraduate degree. The SASS provides a snap-shot of the workforce at a point in time, not a profile over time. To investigate changes in the workforce, we separate full-time public school teachers into two categories: new (less than three years' experience) and experienced. As figure 3.1 shows, there was no pronounced difference between these two groups with respect to the quality of the colleges attended. The proportion of new teachers who graduated from colleges rated selective or above average was slightly higher than the corresponding share among experienced instructors. In the above-average category this difference is statistically significant at 10 percent. However, this artificial "before and after"

Figure 3.1 Changes in the Workforce: College Attended

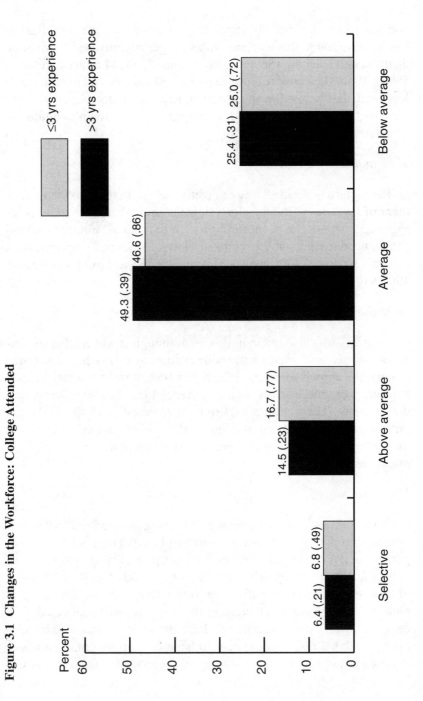

comparison makes no allowance for the effects of attrition. Earlier studies have found that teachers with stronger cognitive skills are more likely to quit teaching (Schlechty and Vance 1981; Murnane and Olsen 1990). If so, the proportion of experienced teachers from better colleges will fall below the share among new instructors, even without increases in pay. Thus the modest "improvement" shown in figure 3.1 overstates the true gain.

Math and Science Teachers

The picture is decidedly more positive when it comes to the recruitment of teachers with bachelor's degrees in mathematics or science. Figure 3.2 shows the proportion of such individuals among new and experienced teachers at the secondary level.[3] Math and science majors rose to 9.9 percent of the new recruits in 1987-88 and to 11.7 percent in 1990-91—statistically significant gains.

Secondary School Instructors with Academic Majors

Progress was also made in this area, though it was neither as dramatic nor as sustained as in the recruitment of math and science majors. As shown in figure 3.2, in 1987-88, new secondary school teachers were more likely than experienced teachers to have an academic major. The trend appears to have reversed in 1990-91, though one should be cautious comparing results across surveys. Changes on the survey format may well have increased the number of miscoded responses.

Undergraduate GPA

Grades of new graduates entering teaching (as reported to the Surveys of Recent College Graduates) are displayed in figure 3.3. The proportion of graduates who by their own report earned mostly A's in college has held steady. The same is largely true of those with lower grades, except for the sharp drop in the 1991 cohort. This drop is almost certainly due to changes in the way data were collected. In a departure from earlier practice, the 1991 survey was conducted by telephone. Inflated responses appear to have been more common under these conditions. A cautious reading of the evidence from the SRCG

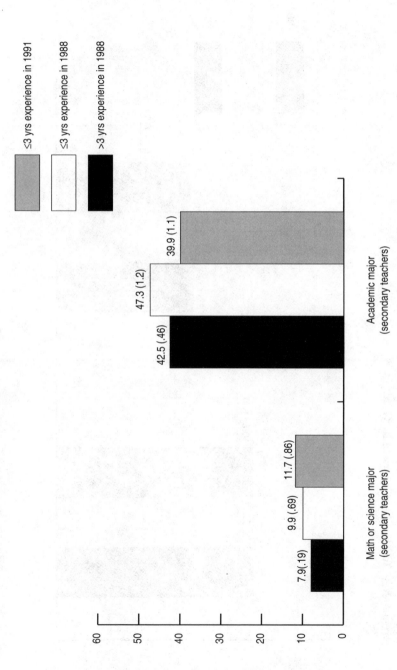

Figure 3.2 Changes in the Workforce: Subject Matter Preparation

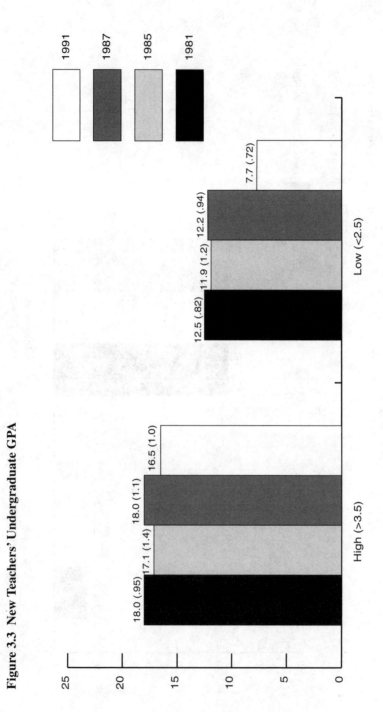

Figure 3.3 New Teachers' Undergraduate GPA

would therefore suggest that little change has occurred in the distribution of grades among new teachers.

To summarize, the evidence reviewed here indicates that the quality of new recruits to teaching improved modestly during the 1980s. The strongest sign of improvement is the rising share of teachers who have majored in mathematics or science. SAT scores have also risen among high school seniors who intend to major in education. Evidence that more secondary school teachers have majored in academic disciplines is weaker, as is the evidence that more teachers attended highly rated colleges and universities. There has been no gain in the proportion of top students, as measured by self-reported GPA, who become public school teachers.

Recruitment and Salaries

None of the analysis to this point indicates whether these changes were caused by increases in salary. To investigate this question, we compare recruitment to salary growth at the state level.

As noted in chapter 1, teacher salaries rose an average of 20 percent after inflation during the 1980s. While this is a substantial real increase, it should be measured against the gains for college-educated workers in general over the same period. Increases were particularly pronounced among women, as entry barriers in other professions continued to fall. Our measure of teacher salaries is therefore the ratio of teacher pay to a gender-weighted average of the earnings of college-educated workers.[4] Even by this measure, teacher salaries rose in all but five states. In most states gains exceeded 10 percent (figure 3.4). More important for our purposes, there was considerable variation across states in real salary growth. This cross-sectional variation furnishes us with an opportunity to see whether improvements in recruitment were associated with higher salaries.

We begin by exploring the relationship between salary changes and the SAT scores of prospective education majors. Since state universities in many western and southern states require the ACT rather than the SAT, skewing the population of SAT examinees, we have restricted the sample to states where at least 40 percent of graduating seniors took the SAT. Figure 3.5 shows that there is essentially no relationship between state-level changes in teacher salaries and SAT scores between 1979 and 1989. Neither is there a strong relationship between salary increases and changes in the share of high school students intending to major in education. The slope of a regression line through the latter data is positive but statistically insignificant (figure 3.6).

Figure 3.4 Changes in Relative Teacher Salaries by State

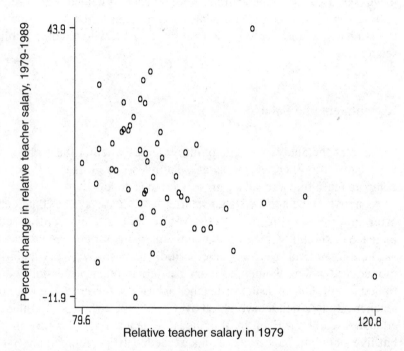

While figure 3.5 seems to show that salary changes are not responsible for test score gains among prospective education majors, this conclusion is valid only to the extent that these students plan to make their careers in their home states. Although we are unable to test this explanation directly, we find that new teachers do not exhibit a great deal of mobility. According to the SRCG, more than 80 percent of newly trained teachers take jobs in the states where they attended college. This fraction is highest among graduates of state universities, lowest

Figure 3.5 Relative SAT Scores of Education Majors and Teacher Pay

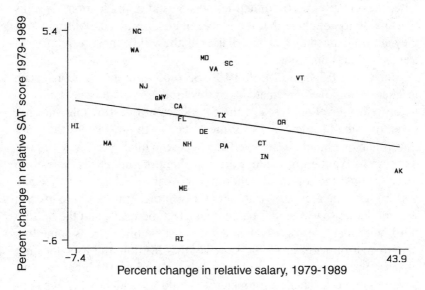

Figure 3.6 Education Majors' Share of SAT Takers and Teacher Pay

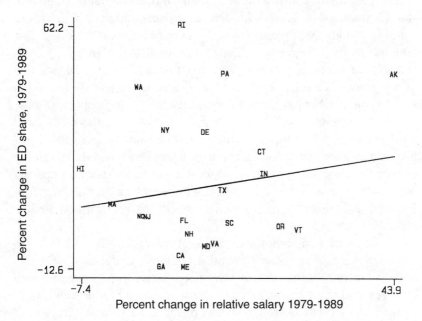

among persons who attended prestigious colleges. Since many of the latter presumably return to their home states after graduation, it seems reasonable to conclude that the career plans of high school seniors, if they are influenced by teacher salaries at all, will be most responsive to trends in their home states.

Since the 1987-88 and 1990-91 SASS report the state in which each teacher is employed, mismatches of this kind are not an issue. Unfortunately, state-level analyses of the SASS are of questionable validity, given the small sample sizes for most states. (In most states there are fewer than one hundred surveyed teachers who qualify as "new" by our definition.) We therefore adopt the expedient of classifying states into three groups: the top third, where the growth in relative teacher pay was highest (increases of 18.6 percent or more), those where growth was moderate (between 8.7 percent and 18.6 percent), and the bottom third, with increases of less than 8.7 percent.[5] While there is some loss of information from grouping states in this fashion, the loss does not obscure the answer to a simple yes or no question. If higher salaries have improved teacher recruitment, it should be evident when we contrast outcomes across these three groups.

The geographical distribution of high-, moderate-, and low-growth states is depicted in figure 3.7. There is a concentration of high-growth states in the northern plains (though lower population density in this area means the geographical distribution of *teachers* in high-growth states is considerably less concentrated). It should be remembered that salary growth is a relative measure, so that states awarding substantial increases in teacher pay are not necessarily high-growth states, if these increases only managed to match gains for other college-educated workers. Although there is some evidence that states in the high-growth category began the decade with lower levels of teacher quality (see below), we implicitly control for such differences by comparing new teachers to experienced teachers within each category. Other confounding influences (e.g., differential rates of teacher attrition) are discussed below.

We begin by revisiting the question of college quality. There is no evidence that raising teacher pay attracted more graduates of selective colleges into teaching (figure 3.8). The relationship between salary changes and the improvement in the workforce is not monotonic. Instead, the moderate-growth states appear to have gained the most.[6]

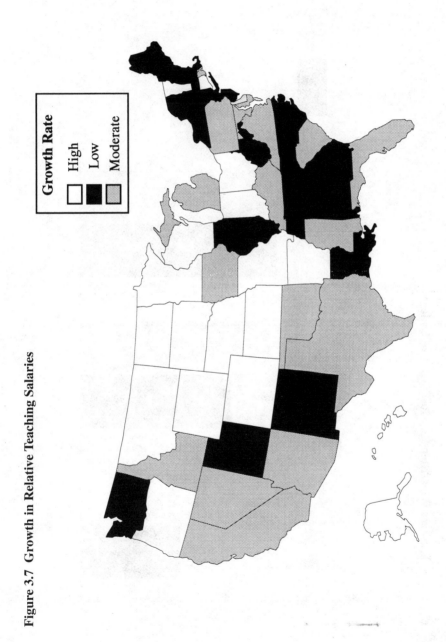

Figure 3.7 Growth in Relative Teaching Salaries

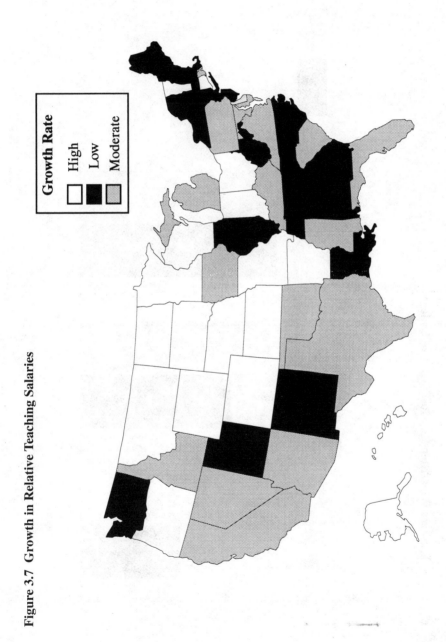

Growth Rate

High
Low
Moderate

25

Figure 3.8 Teachers Who Attended Most Selective Colleges

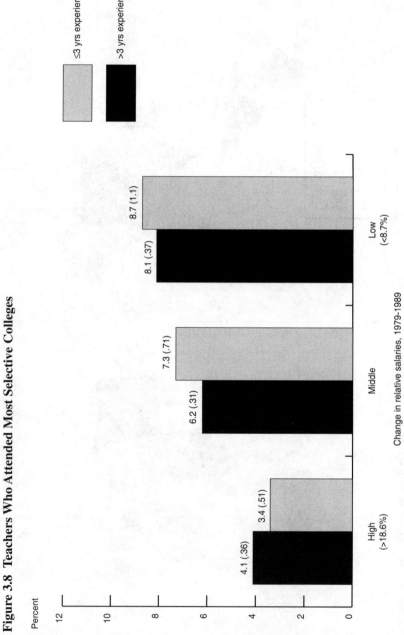

Figure 3.9 Teachers Who Attended Least Selective Colleges

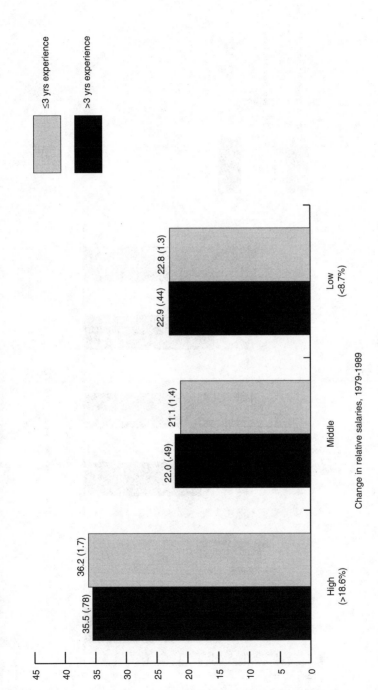

≤3 yrs experience

>3 yrs experience

35.5 (.78)   36.2 (1.7)   22.0 (.49)   21.1 (1.4)   22.9 (.44)   22.8 (1.3)

High
(>18.6%)

Middle

Low
(<8.7%)

Change in relative salaries, 1979-1989

45   40   35   30   25   20   15   10   5   0

Figure 3.10 Secondary School Teachers with Bachelor's Degrees in Math or Science

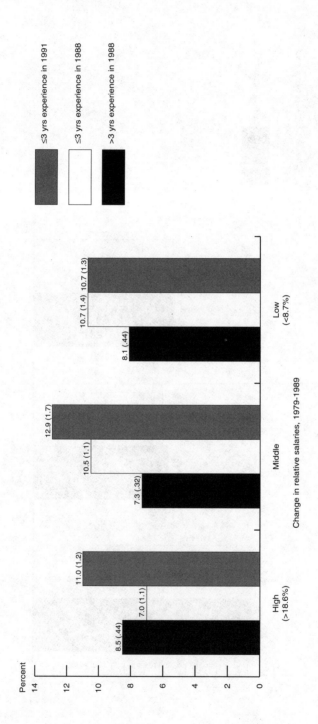

Legend:
- ≤3 yrs experience in 1991
- ≤3 yrs experience in 1988
- >3 yrs experience in 1988

High (>18.6%): 8.5 (.44), 7.0 (1.1), 11.0 (1.2)

Middle: 7.3 (.32), 10.5 (1.1), 12.9 (1.7)

Low (<8.7%): 8.1 (.44), 10.7 (1.4), 10.7 (1.3)

Percent: 0, 2, 4, 6, 8, 10, 12, 14

Change in relative salaries, 1979-1989

Similar remarks apply to other indicators of quality: graduates of the least selective colleges (figure 3.9), teachers with math and science degrees (figure 3.10), and instructors with academic majors (figure 3.11). In none of these cases do the data support the hypothesis that improvements in teacher recruitment, such as they are, have resulted from salary increases.[7]

The absence of any relationship between salary changes and the quality of new recruits is surprising, though it is not difficult to find other explanations for the modest improvement among new teacher recruits in the 1980s. These include the wide publicity given an impending "teacher shortage," a signal that job opportunities were about to increase. In addition, many states and districts placed new emphasis on recruiting teachers with better subject area preparation. Still, our negative finding is so unsuspected that it is worth pausing to consider whether it could be due to limitations of the data or faulty analysis. We discuss two of the more likely possibilities.

Measurement Error in Salaries

Average teaching salaries at the state level are compiled by the National Education Association from a survey of State Departments of Education. These state-level averages reflect changes in the composition of the workforce. This means that measured salary is not a pure price. Since teachers are rewarded for education and experience, a shift toward more experienced and better-educated teachers can cause average pay to rise even when there has been no change in underlying salary schedules. Thus part of the variation in state salaries may be irrelevant to career decisions, if the latter depend on salary schedule *levels* as opposed to movements along given schedules.

Changes in teachers' experience and education are not easily obtained at the state level, making it difficult to remove these effects from the salary series. However, since the SASS was administered twice, first in 1987-88 and again in 1990-91, it is possible to examine the sources of salary growth between those years. As shown in appendix 3B, 95 percent of the variation in state-level salary growth between these years can be explained by upward shifts in schedules. (Changes in the education and experience of states' teachers alone explain no more than 20 percent of this variation.) Unless these three years are

Figure 3.11 Secondary School Teachers with Academic Majors

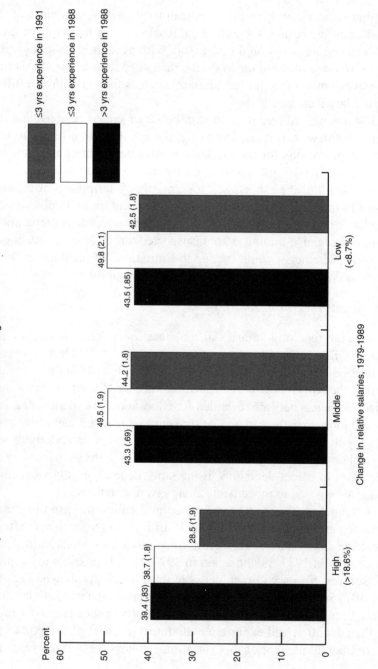

Percent

≤3 yrs experience in 1991
≤3 yrs experience in 1988
>3 yrs experience in 1988

High
(>18.6%)

39.4 (.83)
38.7 (1.8)
28.5 (1.9)

Middle

43.3 (.69)
49.5 (1.9)
44.2 (1.8)

Low
(<8.7%)

43.5 (.85)
49.8 (2.1)
42.5 (1.8)

Change in relative salaries, 1979-1989

highly atypical, it is therefore quite unlikely that our three-way classification of states by salary growth would be altered in any significant
way by taking into account teachers' accumulation of additional
degrees and experience.

A rise in the salary schedule need not occur evenly. Some districts
may award larger raises to starting teachers (frontloading); in other districts, experienced teachers may benefit most (backloading). Since new
teachers are presumably not indifferent to the distribution of increases
over the life cycle, state average pay may not accurately capture the
incentives they face.

Unfortunately, there is little hard evidence about the extent of backloading. Detailed analysis has been done for only a few states. Jacobson (1988) and Lankford and Wyckoff (1994) found that most districts
in New York State have backloaded teachers' raises over the past
twenty-five years. According to an analysis of district pay scales in
Michigan, during the economic decline of the 1970s and early 1980s,
salaries offered beginning teachers fell more (in percentage terms) than
did salaries at the top of the schedules (Murnane et al. 1987). However,
when district salaries were weighted by the number of teachers
employed, no such pattern was evident.

Even if more data on the prevalence of backloading were readily
available, we strongly suspect it would not make any great difference
to the analysis here. Backloading matters only to the extent that its
incidence varies systematically across high-, moderate-, and low-
growth states. Thus, if high-growth states also practiced more backloading, this might account for the fact that teacher recruitment in these
states improved no more than it did elsewhere. In fact, since backloading appears to result from the influence of strong teacher unions on
contracts, it is likely that precisely the opposite relationship holds. An
inspection of figure 3.7 shows that many of the low-growth states (New
York, New Jersey, Illinois) have strong teacher unions, while high- and
moderate-growth states are concentrated in regions with weaker
unions.

Job Growth in Undesirable Locations

Success in recruiting new teachers depends not just on salary but
also on working conditions in the schools where vacancies occur.

When job openings are concentrated in less-desirable school systems, recruitment will suffer. Perhaps, then, salary growth was greatest where new jobs were hardest to fill.

To explore this hypothesis, we compare the characteristics of districts in which new and experienced teachers worked. These characteristics include the percentage of students at each school eligible for free or reduced-price lunch (a proxy for the poverty rate), the percentage of black and Hispanic students, and indicators of a less-desirable location (urban or rural as opposed to small town or suburb). We also compare salaries of teachers with a BA and no experience to see whether job openings have been concentrated among poorer-paying districts.

The comparison of experienced to new teachers in the 1987-88 SASS shows that experienced teachers were, indeed, more likely to hold jobs in districts with attractive characteristics (table 3.1). It does not appear, however, that this pattern varies systematically with salary growth. For example, the gap between new and experienced teachers with respect to poverty rates and the percentage of minority students at their schools was greatest in the moderate growth states which enjoyed, by and large, the largest improvement in teacher recruitment.

Compared to the 1987-88 workforce, new teachers in 1990-91 were somewhat more likely to work in districts with high poverty rates, less likely to take jobs in schools with high percentages of minority students. These differences probably reflect economic recession and demographic changes in student enrollments, since the same trends are apparent among experienced teachers. However, some statistics offer support for the hypothesis under consideration. New teachers in low salary growth states were less likely to hold jobs in large central city school systems than were experienced teachers in the same states. In addition, while new teachers were more often employed in rural districts in all three categories, the percentage was particularly high (compared to experienced teachers) in those states with the highest rates of salary growth. If inner city and rural jobs are less attractive, states with high salary growth may have been at a relative disadvantage in filling vacant positions.

The disadvantage is unlikely to have had a pronounced effect on our findings, as a few calculations will show. First, the difference between the shares of new teachers and experienced teachers in rural districts never exceeds more than about 10 percentage points. Even if a rural

Table 3.1 Characteristics of School Systems in which New and Experienced Teachers Work

	Exper. 87-88			New 87-88			Exper. 90-91			New 90-91		
	High	Mid	Low	High	Mid	Low	High	Mid	Low	High	Mid	Low
Poverty rate	23.8	29.0	28.4	27.4	32.9	30.0	25.9	33.9	31.8	30.7	39.7	35.0
	(.48)	(.55)	(.55)	(1.1)	(.93)	(1.1)	(.67)	(.81)	(.56)	(.95)	(1.2)	(1.3)
Percent black & Hispanic	14.1	32.9	29.0	16.0	37.6	30.2	12.7	21.5	25.3	14.0	36.3	25.7
	(.48)	(.57)	(.55)	(.83)	(1.2)	(1.5)	(.51)	(.74)	(.57)	(1.7)	(1.1)	(1.4)
Large city	2.8	7.3	8.0	3.2	7.8	8.9	---	---	---	---	---	---
	(.37)	(.42)	(.43)	(1.1)	(1.1)	(1.1)						
Mid-sized city	7.9	10.1	9.0	6.2	8.7	8.9	---	---	---	---	---	---
	(.45)	(.64)	(.52)	(.77)	(.98)	(1.2)						
Large central city	---	---	---	---	---	---	5.5	11.7	13.3	5.7	13.0	8.1
							(.64)	(.60)	(.77)	(1.2)	(1.0)	(1.6)
Mid-sized central city	---	---	---	---	---	---	17.0	17.8	14.0	14.	18.3	15.4
							(.75)	(.72)	(.63)	(1.4)	(1.3)	(1.7)
Rural	30.5	22.3	19.0	39.9	24.3	25.2	26.2	16.1	16.0	38.2	16.9	21.1
	(1.2)	(.74)	(.73)	(1.9)	(1.5)	(1.6)	(.93)	(.55)	(.76)	(1.6)	(1.1)	(1.7)
Starting pay ($1,000)	17.5	18.3	18.9	17.3	18.2	19.1	20.0	22.0	21.7	19.8	21.9	20.8
	(.03)	(.04)	(.04)	(.07)	(.07)	(.07)	(.05)	(.08)	(.08)	(.12)	(.11)	(.13)

SOURCE: *Schools and Staffing Surveys*, 1987-88 and 1990-91. Experienced teachers in 1987-88 = more than three years' experience; in 1990-91, more than six years' experience. New teachers = three or fewer years' experience in both samples. Standard errors in parentheses.

teacher is only half as likely to be of high quality (by whatever indicator), the difference would cause the representation of high-quality teachers in the new workforce (vis-a-vis the experienced workforce) to fall by only 5 percent (= 50 percent of .10). This would reduce their share of the workforce from, say, 20 percent to 19 percent. Thus, the fact that more job opportunities in high-growth states arose in rural districts would have, by itself, only a very small effect on the measured quality of new recruits. Moreover, this illustrative calculation probably overstates the true impact. The incidence of most of our quality indicators varies only slightly from rural to nonrural districts: ratios are nearer 1:1 than 1:2. Recruitment effects involving such minute fractions of the workforce cannot explain our findings.

We note finally that there are virtually no differences between experienced and new teachers with respect to district starting salaries. New teachers have not been channeled into jobs in the lowest-paying districts.

Teacher Salaries and the Ratings Principals Give Their Staffs

It remains possible, of course, that higher salaries have improved teacher recruitment in ways unrelated to these indicators of teacher quality. As noted in chapter 2, the 1990-91 SASS requested principals to rate the quality of their teaching staffs on a five-point scale (poor = 1, excellent = 5). Principals were free to evaluate teachers by whatever criteria they chose and presumably selected those most relevant to the needs of their schools as they saw them. A particularly valuable feature of the survey was the inclusion of separate ratings for experienced teachers (more than three years' experience) and new staff.

Overall, experienced teachers received higher ratings than new staff. The question of interest is whether the difference diminishes in states that raised salaries the most. Figure 3.12 depicts the ratings of new and experienced staff, by state salary growth. While ratings given experienced staff were quite similar across all three groups, new teachers were, indeed, more likely to be rated "excellent" in states with high salary growth.

Since ratings were obtained from each school in the SASS, it is possible to explore this relationship in greater detail. We estimate two models. In the first, the ratings given new teachers are assumed to be a

Figure 3.12 Principals' Ratings of Their Staffs, by Salary Growth

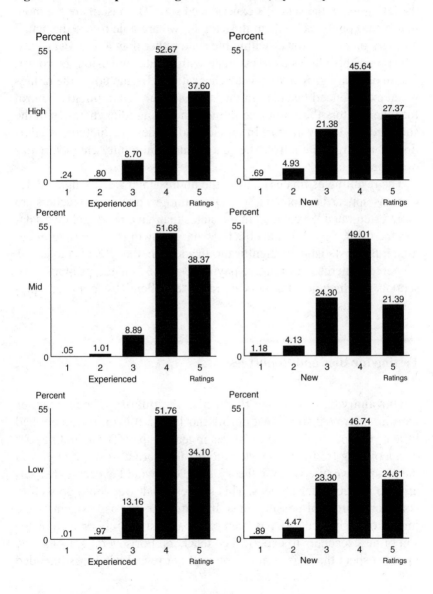

function of the relative growth of teacher salaries at the state level and the rating given the school's experienced staff. Because there are more than 8,000 public schools in the sample, we are able to use the actual measure of salary growth within the state rather than a three-way classification. This allows us to estimate with greater precision the contribution of salary growth to new teacher ratings. By including the ratings given experienced teachers in the same school, we implicitly control for other factors that influence ratings, including idiosyncrasies in the standards of the evaluator. In our second model, we include as additional background controls the school and community characteristics examined in table 3.1.

The resulting estimates confirm the impression given by figure 3.12. (Details appear in appendix 3C.) Other things equal, new teachers are more often rated "excellent" in the states that have raised relative salaries the most. Yet while the effect of salary growth is in the right direction, it is not statistically significant. In addition, the effect is modest. A 20 percent increase in relative pay raises the estimated proportion of schools in which new teachers are rated "excellent" by less than 2 percentage points.

Testing for Bias and Robustness

Our analysis has shown that while the quality of new teacher recruits improved somewhat during the 1980s, this improvement had little or nothing to do with increases in teacher pay. These findings are disappointing from a policy standpoint. They are also surprising from the perspective of economic theory, since one would expect higher salaries to affect career choices. This suggests that we would do well to consider sources of possible bias. In particular, our assessment of the impact of higher salaries has been based almost entirely on a comparison of new teachers to experienced teachers. For several reasons, one might suspect that this comparison will not reveal what it is intended to.

Resumed Careers

Our experienced teacher category has included persons who recently resumed teaching careers. If higher salaries induced these persons to take up teaching again, it would make more sense to group returning teachers with new entrants into the profession. To see whether this matters, we reclassify former teachers who reentered the profession after 1984 as "new" teachers.[8] This change has virtually no effect on the measured incidence of our quality indicators. Our analysis continues to show as much improvement in states with low and moderate salary growth as in states where teacher pay rose the most.

Cohort Effects

Many experienced instructors started teaching well before the decline in teacher salaries during the late 1970s. Since these persons might not resemble teachers who entered when salaries were low, their inclusion with other experienced teachers skews the comparison we wish to make. A fairer test would exclude them.

Unfortunately, the data do not allow us to construct precisely this comparison group. Instead, we exclude all persons who had ten or more years' experience in 1987-88. This will screen out most teachers who began their careers before the downturn in salaries. Moreover, those who slip through this screen are unlikely to have begun teaching much earlier than the mid-70s, since relatively few persons return to teaching after long interruptions (Murnane et al. 1991).

This change has a substantial effect on only one indicator, the percentage of experienced secondary school teachers with an academic major, which falls by 3 to 5 percentage points. Since the magnitude of this decline is independent of salary growth, our earlier conclusions stand.

Out of State Recruits

Teachers may move from states that have not raised pay to those that have. If better teachers tend to be more mobile, the quality of the experienced workforce rises in the recipient state and falls in the donor state. Both responses obscure the consequences of salary growth by shifting the quality of the experienced workforce in the same hypothesized direction as the quality of new recruits.

It turns out, however, that the number of teachers who move across state boundaries is too small to affect our findings. Fewer than 2 percent of the experienced teachers in 1987-88 gave up a teaching position in another state to begin their current jobs. Moreover, this figure includes all moves, not merely those subsequent to the onset of salary reforms. When we test the explanatory power of this hypothesis by excluding out-of-state movers from the comparison groups, there are virtually no changes in the values of our quality indicators.

Attrition Bias

Higher pay lowers attrition. If better teachers are more sensitive to salary levels in deciding whether to quit, their share of the experienced workforce will rise. This, of course, makes it more difficult to detect a relative improvement in the quality of new recruits.

Could this explain why high growth states do not appear to have had more success recruiting new teachers? Note that our experienced teachers were all hired before the 1985-86 school year. For salary reforms that began in the early 1980s to have much impact on the composition of this group via differential attrition, quit rates of better teachers must be considerably more salary-sensitive than those of other instructors. Yet Murnane and Olsen (1990) found that the exit decisions of North Carolina teachers with high scores on the National Teachers Examination were actually less responsive to salary than were the decisions of teachers with lower scores. Our own investigation of data from the SASS Teacher Follow-Up Survey finds no statistically significant difference between the exit elasticities of teachers who attended selective colleges and others (Ballou and Podgursky 1993a).

In addition, attrition among experienced teachers is not very large. Even if wage elasticities did vary by teacher quality, the base quit rate is too low to produce a significant impact on the workforce in a span of three to four years.

Omitted Policy Variables

Pay raises were not the only education reforms undertaken during the 1980s. Many states also raised standards for teacher training and certification. Thus states that did not increase salaries may have improved recruitment through other means. This would be particularly likely if policy makers tended to view pay raises and higher standards as alternatives, with some states choosing the first route, others the second.

Several states now require that secondary school teachers have an undergraduate major in their principal subject area (NASDTEC 1991). To see whether the impact of this change could be confounded with that of salary growth, we sort states into two new classifications, those where such a requirement was in place in 1990-91, and the rest. Although salary growth was somewhat higher among the latter, the difference was not great (13 percent versus 10 percent). Thus it does not appear that salary reforms/higher standards constituted an either-or choice. Just as important, these requirements have had little effect on the qualifications of new teachers. The percentage of new secondary school teachers in the 1990-91 SASS who majored in an academic subject in college was virtually identical across the two groups: 41.6 percent and 41.5 percent, respectively. Whether this is the result of weak enforcement or the slow phasing-in of new requirements, it does not appear that omitting this policy reform from the analysis has biased our earlier findings.

We also test whether our results are sensitive to changes in classification schemes and definitions. We begin with salary growth. In our first test, teacher salaries are measured relative to a simple average (not a gender-weighted average) of the salaries of college graduates. This has little effect on measured growth rates. As a second alternative, we measure the growth in teacher salaries relative to the national Consumer Price Index. These calculations are of particular interest if the decision to enter teaching is based not on a comparison of relative earnings but on the ability to attain a target standard of living. Measuring the growth in teaching salaries this way considerably alters the classification of states by "high," "moderate," and "low" rates of salary growth. However, there is still no evidence that high growth states have systematically outperformed others.

Reverting to the original measure of relative salary, we alter the end-points of the interval over which we measure salary changes, in the one case using 1978 and 1990, in the other, 1980 and 1988.[9] These changes make only slight differences to our results. Next, we restrict the category of new teachers in 1987-88 to persons with no more than two years' experience. We then expand this category to include persons with four years' experience. Finally, we restrict the experienced group to persons with seven or more years' experience in 1990-91.

Results are generally quite robust to these respecifications. In the few cases where measures of teacher quality change significantly, these changes do not systematically favor the high growth states.

Conclusion

The evidence reviewed here indicates that the quality of new recruits to teaching improved during the 1980s. SAT scores rose among high school seniors intending to major in education. New teachers hired during this decade were more likely to have majored in an academic subject, especially mathematics or science. However, there was little if any gain by other indicators, among them teachers' undergraduate GPA and the quality of the colleges they attended.

These improvements do not appear to be related to salary increases. By virtually all indicators, progress has been independent of the rate of salary growth at the state level. The single exception is provided by principals' ratings of the staffs in the 1990-91 Schools and Staffing Survey. Even in this case, however, the practical import of this relationship is limited: a 20 percent increase in teachers' salaries raises the share of schools with "excellent" new teachers by less than 2 percentage points—a statistically insignificant effect.

We have subjected our findings to a number of specification tests. The results indicate that our conclusions are not the result of obvious biases that might have affected the statistical analysis. Our findings also appear to be robust to alternative measurements of salary trends and to various ways of defining who is to be counted as an experienced teacher or a new teacher.

It is possible, of course, that better analytical techniques might detect a positive relationship between salary growth and the quality of new teachers. In particular, it might be wondered if we have not placed too much emphasis on state variation in salary growth. After all, prospective teachers may have responded to salary growth in other states, anticipating that their own state would follow. If so, the national trend in teacher pay may have had an important influence on career decisions. This argument could also account for the fact that the quality of newly recruited teachers improved nationwide during the 1980s.

There may be some truth to this claim, but we do not believe it provides an adequate explanation for the near absence of a correlation at the state level between salary growth and improvements in the workforce. Even if prospective teachers thought it likely that their state would match the growth in salaries elsewhere, one would still expect an actual boost in pay to carry more weight than one that remained speculative. Moreover, as time passed, it became clear that not all states were acting in the same manner.

As for the improvement in teacher quality nationwide, alternative explanations seem more compelling. In the first place, the job market improved for teachers during the 1980s. Indeed, there was a well-publicized threat of a teacher shortage that probably led many to believe it would be easier to find a teaching job than it proved to be. In addition, by the end of this decade, virtually all states had raised standards for admission to teacher education programs and teacher certification. Finally, public education received a great deal of attention in the national media. This may have influenced career decisions.

This is not to say that the analysis presented here will have satisfied all skeptics. However, we do not believe that much can be gained by sifting the data further in an effort to confirm or refute our conclusions. Rather, we would argue that our findings raise, at the very least, serious doubts about the policy many states have followed. Certainly it would be unwise simply to assume that raising pay will improve teacher quality. That it should be so difficult to detect any gains from the salary increases of the 1980s suggests that we need to take a closer look at what happens in teacher labor markets when salaries rise.

NOTES

1. Results of this kind have been found in studies using measures of teacher quality similar to ours (Ehrenberg and Brewer 1994; Ferguson 1991; Chambers 1985). Estimates of hedonic wage equations for teachers have also shown that teachers with more coursework in their subject areas (Smith and Lee 1990) and higher scores on a test of verbal ability (Antos and Rosen 1975) earn more, though the returns are quite modest.(For example, Antos and Rosen found that teachers who missed 50 percent or more of the test questions earned almost as much (96 percent) as higher-scoring instructors.) Other research has explored the relationship between teacher salaries and students' educational outcomes. These studies form part of a much larger literature that debates the relationship between spending on education and educational outcomes; much of this literature yields negative conclusions. For a review, see Hanushek (1986).

2. This is not to say that only and all of those high school seniors who intend to major in education will ultimately become teachers. Indeed, evidence from the National Longitudinal Survey of 1972 reveals that many of these persons pursued other careers, while many who had different plans in high school became teachers, at least for a time (Vance and Schlechty 1982). Nonetheless, even though final career decisions are uncertain, changes in board scores should signal whether higher salaries have led better students to consider careers in education.

3. We express math and science majors as a percentage of all secondary school teachers, not as a percentage of those teaching math or science, since the number of math and science teachers is strongly influenced by policies governing the assignment of teachers outside their areas of certification. In any event, if there is excess demand for such personnel, a simple measure of their representation in the workforce should indicate whether recruitment has improved.

4. To obtain these figures, average teachers salaries in each state were divided by a weighted average of the earnings of full-time workers with four years of college, as reported in the decennial census (published statistics for 1980, 5 percent public use sample for 1990). Since teacher contracts typically run from September to September, academic years 1978-79 and 1988-89 provide the greatest overlap with the periods covered by the census (incomes for 1979 and 1989, respectively). Teacher salaries are from the *Digest of Education Statistics*. Weights are derived from the 1987-88 Schools and Staffing Survey and reflect the proportions of men and women in the teaching force of each state in that year.

5. To facilitate comparisons, this tripartite classification is based on relative salary changes from school years 1978-79 to 1988-89, even though the first SASS was conducted in 1987. The ranking of states as "high," "middle," or "low" is virtually the same when based on salary changes through 1987, leaving our conclusions unaltered.

6. Recall that data on teachers' undergraduate colleges are available for the 1987-88 school years but not for 1990-91. One might wonder if 1987 was too soon after the onset of salary reform for a response to be apparent. Fortunately, recently released data from the Schools and Staffing Survey of 1993-94 allow us to check this possibility, since the item on teachers' undergraduate colleges was restored in the 1992-94 SASS. Although these data arrived too late for us to include a full analysis of them in this monograph, we have used them to explore the possibility that improvement appeared with a lag.

Following the analysis for earlier years, we distinguish teachers who were new in 1993-94 (no more than three years' experience) from those who were experienced. There is no evidence that states that boosted pay the most over the 1980s benefited from a lagged effect on recruitment in the early 1990s. For example, among high-growth states, teachers from selective colleges made up 5.1 percent of the new workforce, compared to 4.2 percent of the experienced workforce. But the difference was just as great in the states with moderate salary growth and substantially greater in states with low salary growth, where 11.7 percent of new teachers came from these colleges, compared to 7.2 percent of the experienced workforce. (Omitted from this analysis are teachers who graduated from colleges not in the 1987-88 analysis; this is, however, a negligible proportion of the workforce, comprising for the most part graduates of foreign universities or small, obscure American colleges.)

As an alternative check on our findings, we dispense with the new/experienced breakdown and simply compare the 1993-94 workforce to the 1987-88 workforce. We find very little change in the composition of the workforce. Two statistics indicate a positive relationship between salary changes and teacher quality. Among states with low salary growth, the share of teachers from selective colleges fell from 8.8 to 7.7 percent (significant at 10 percent). In high-growth states, the proportion of the workforce from above-average colleges grew from 12.3 to 13.7 percent (significant at 5 percent). There were no other statistically significant changes. Overall there was very little alteration in the makeup of the workforce between the two surveys. And, of course, these changes take everything into account: retirement, in-migration, and retention, as well as recruitment of new graduates.

7. Because the samples are smaller and more sensitive to sample design, we do not report a comparable breakdown on GPA data from the SRCG. Our attempts to conduct such an analysis found that statistics fluctuated implausibly with small changes in the classification of states as "high," "middle," or "low," and in the period over which relative salary changes are measured. This was not the case with the data from the SASS.

8. By "former teachers" we mean persons who took up another occupation during the intervening years. This includes homemakers but not persons who attended school, since many teachers who study during leaves or sabbaticals are pursuing professional development and intend to return to teaching afterward.

9. For this purpose, we extrapolate earnings of college graduates at the state level beyond the census year. Extrapolation is based on the rate of change of earnings at the state-level from *Employment and Earnings, Annual State Averages.* These data represent earnings of all types of workers, college-educated and noncollege-educated alike. Nonetheless, year-to-year changes should reflect local differences in economic conditions affecting economic prospects for all residents of the state.

Appendix 3A
Data Sources

The principal sources of data for this study were the two Schools and Staffing Surveys, conducted during the 1987-88 and 1990-91 academic years, and the series of Surveys of Recent College Graduates, conducted in 1976, 1978, 1981, 1985, and 1991. The purpose of this appendix is not to provide an exhaustive description of these data, but rather to highlight features of these data sources of particular importance for this study. Readers desiring more information about either series may wish to consult the following publications of the National Center for Education Statistics: Choy et al., *Schools and Staffing in the United States: A Statistical Profile, 1987-88* (NCES 92-120); Choy et al., *Schools and Staffing in the United States: A Statistical Profile, 1990-91* (NCES 93-146); Frankel and Stowe, *New Teachers in the Job Market, 1987 Update* (NCES 90-336).

The Schools and Staffing Surveys

Each Schools and Staffing Survey comprised four questionnaires: (1) a district (LEA) questionnaire, sent to approximately 5500 public school district offices chosen through stratified sampling; (2) a school questionnaire, sent to selected schools within these districts; (3) an administrator questionnaire, sent to the principal or headmaster of each of these schools; (4) a teacher questionnaire, sent to several teachers at these schools. The number of teachers selected was a function of school size and grade level. On average, four to six teachers were sampled per school. For stand-alone private schools, the 1987-88 district questionnaire was also sent to the school. In the 1990-91 SASS, the district and school questionnaires were collapsed into one.

In both years surveys were sent to more than 9,000 public and 3,000 private schools. Response rates were high, averaging more than 90 percent of public schools and 80 percent of private schools. Just over 56,000 public school teachers were surveyed in each year. The 1987-88 sample of private school teachers was slightly larger, at 11,529, than was the 1990-91 survey, at 9,166. Response rates among teachers ranged between 80 and 90 percent.

In 1987-88 the teacher questionnaire obtained information on the institution that awarded the teacher's undergraduate degree and the major program of study. The first of these items was dropped from the 1990-91 survey. No information was obtained on other measures of academic achievement, such as undergraduate grades and test scores.

In chapter 3 we assess the effect of salary increases on recruitment by comparing the characteristics of new public school teachers to those of experienced teachers. Full-time teachers only are used, thus excluding part-time instructors and persons who served part-time as administrators. Unfortunately, the number of new teachers surveyed in a given state tended to be small (often less than 100). As a result, state-level aggregates are far too noisy to conduct analysis at this level. Instead, we group states into those that experienced high growth, moderate growth, and low growth in teacher salaries.

The school component of the SASS provides information on student and community characteristics, which we use as indicators of job attractiveness in table 3.1.

We also make considerable use of the SASS in chapter 6, to compare compensation and personnel policies across public and private schools. On virtually every point of interest, inconsistencies in the items covered between survey years generally prevented us from pooling data from the two surveys. Even so, estimates are generally precise enough to provide a clear picture of differences between the two sectors.

Surveys of Recent College Graduates

Six surveys were conducted at irregular intervals between the years 1976 and 1991. Surveys were conducted in spring of the year following graduation. Thus, respondents to the 1976 survey were individuals who graduated between July 1, 1974 and June 30, 1975. Only recipients of bachelor's and master's degrees were surveyed. Our analysis uses responses of the former. The number of respondents varied from a low of 4,350 in the first year of the survey to a high of 17,276 in 1987. Teachers were oversampled, since a principal purpose of these surveys was to investigate the flow of newly trained teachers onto the job market.

The SRCG sample was obtained first by selecting a group of colleges and universities, who provided a list of recent graduates from which the survey sample was chosen. In 1987 and 1991, for example, 400 institutions were chosen. Earlier waves of the survey used fewer schools. As a result of this survey design, the SRCG samples exhibit strong effects of clustering. Changes in the list of institutions surveyed can have a considerable impact on statistics computed from the data. One must be very cautious in interpreting trends in the data for graduates who have come from a small set of schools. Statistics like the proportion of newly trained teachers who graduated from selective colleges are entirely unreliable at the state level; even for groups of states, estimates are sensitive to the way the group is defined (for example, states experiencing high growth in teacher pay). Because the estimates are not robust to fairly minor changes in the composition of groups, we do not report data from the SRCG at this level.

Undergraduate GPA is self-reported on an interval scale, giving rise to questions about its reliability on two counts. Of the two problems, the one stemming from recall bias (or a tendency to enhance one's self-image) appears to be greater than the measurement error induced by mapping interval responses back onto a four-point scale. Access to transcript data for the 1987 survey cohort made it possible to check the accuracy of these self-reported data. We found a pronounced upward bias (except, of course, for the very best students, who could not overstate their grades). This effect was greater, the lower a student's actual grades. As a result, two sorts of measurement error are present. Imprecision in the responses, particularly when converted to a numerical four-point scale, creates a classical errors-in-variables problem, tending to lower the coefficient on GPA in a regression analysis. However, the fact that the measurement error is largely one-sided and inversely correlated with true GPA imparts an offsetting bias. Analyses of the effects of GPA (and other individual attributes) on subsequent earnings, one using reported GPA, the other actual GPA, showed that these effects were almost exactly offsetting, at least in this particular context.

There were many inconsistencies in the wording of survey items and the coding of responses from one survey to the next. We briefly review those which were most important for this study.

In all years but one (1985), new graduates were asked if they had earned a teaching certificate and, if not, whether they were eligible for a certificate (meaning, presumably, that they had completed the necessary course work and student teaching). In 1985 survey subjects were asked only if they were certified or eligible for certification; consequently, we have collapsed the two into a single category in order to preserve consistency of the data across all survey years. Where we write of "certified graduates," it should be understood that it includes persons who may not hold a certificate. This slight ambiguity should not cause great concern, however, since those with certificates are by far the larger group. The 1991 survey, for example, found 3,111 certified graduates and only 127 additional persons who indicated they were eligible but not certified.

Graduates who were certified or eligible for certification were also asked whether they had applied for a teaching job since or just prior to graduating. They were not asked whether this was their first choice or whether they had turned down a teaching position to take a preferred job or to continue their education. In order to avoid false inferences that might arise from taking this response at face-value, we have used other survey items to determine whether an individual was likely to have turned down a teaching position, as explained in chapter 4.

The SRCG inquired whether a teacher worked in a public or a private school and what grade levels and subjects were taught. Otherwise, no information was obtained about school characteristics or even school location. Indeed, in only about one-half of the survey years was the state in which the respondent worked reported. In other years, only the location of the college they had attended was available. To preserve consistency across survey years, college location is therefore used to place graduates within a state or region. Statements in the text about new graduates' mobility are based on an analysis of the surveys that reported both college and job location.

Survey Design

Both the SASS and SRCG sampling designs exhibit stratification and clustering. The SASS particularly oversampled small schools and rural schools. In addition, the SRCG is a choice-based sample, since new graduates who had completed a program of teacher education were more likely to be surveyed. Except where otherwise noted, all statistics reported in this book are computed using sampling weights equal to the inverse probability of selection

Standard errors calculated on the assumption of simple random sampling are biased if observations from the same stratum or cluster exhibit residual correlation. In complex survey designs, it is difficult to specify apriori the covariance matrix of the observations. Instead, resampling techniques can be used to estimate standard errors of parameter estimates. For statistics obtained from the Schools and Staffing Surveys, we use the method of balanced repeated replications (Wolter 1985). The only exception is table 6.7, where we report standard errors obtained from the conventional weighted least squares formula. Levels of statistical significance are so great in this table that allowing for design effects or heteroscedasticity would not change any of our inferences.

For various reasons, some rather technical, it was not possible to follow the same procedure for statistics obtained from the Surveys of Recent College Graduates. Standard errors reported in chapter 4 are obtained from the weighted information matrix for maximum likelihood estimates (under the assumption of independent observations) or, in the case of linear models, the heteroscedasticity-consistent covariance matrix estimator described in White (1980). These estimates of standard errors are likely to be biased downward. This is not as great a cause for concern as might initially appear. Most of our findings are negative in character—that is, variables that one would have expected to matter are not found to have a statistically significant influence on outcomes of interest. This would not change if standard errors were corrected for downward bias. In addition, we are careful not to place great weight in our argument on statistical results of marginal significance.

Appendix 3B
Components of State-Level Salary Growth

We begin our analysis of state-level changes in teacher salaries by specifying a micro-level model of teacher pay:

$$(1) \quad w_{ist} = b_{st} + b_{1t} \, NOBA_{ist} + b_{2t} \, MA_{ist} + b_{3t} \, MAPLUS_{ist}$$
$$+ b_{4t} \, EXPER_{ist} + e_{ist}$$

where w_{ist} is the annual base salary received by teacher i in state s and year t, and

NOBA	= 1 if the teacher does not hold a bachelor's degree;
	= 0 otherwise
MA	= 1 if the teacher's holds a master's degree, but nothing higher;
	= 0 otherwise
MAPLUS	= 1 if the teacher holds a degree above the master's level;
	= 0 otherwise
EXPER	= years of teaching experience, if < 20;
	= 20 if years of experience ≥20

EXPER is censored at 20 since salary schedules commonly top out after 15-20 years of service.

Equation (1) is estimated by ordinary least squares with data from the 1987-88 SASS and from the 1990-91 SASS. These results can be used to express mean teacher pay in each state as

$$(2) \quad W_{s,87} = b_{s,87} + B_{87} \, X_{s,87}$$

and

$$W_{s,90} = b_{s,90} + B_{90} \, X_{s,90}$$

in which X_s represents the mean of the regressor vector for state S and B_t the vector of coefficients in year t. Mean salary growth between 1987 and 1990 can therefore be decomposed into changes in state intercepts, teacher education and experience, and coefficients on education and experience:

$$W_{s,90} - W_{s,87} = (b_{s,90} - b_{s,87}) + B_{90} \, (X_{s,90} - X_{s,87}) + (B_{90} - B_{87}) \, X_{s,87}.$$

Of the three components on the right-hand side of this decomposition, the change in state means has by far the greatest explanatory power. A regression of mean salary changes on the change in state intercepts yields an R^2 of .95. This increases to .98 when the second term is added to the model; however, a regression of mean salary changes on $(X_{s,90}-X_{s,87})$ alone explains only 20 percent of the variation in $W_{s,90} - W_{s,87}$. We conclude that our three-way classification of states would scarcely be affected if we were to control for state-level changes in teacher experience and education.

These results also indicate that by far the greater part of the increase in average teacher pay between 1987 and 1990 resulted from upward shifts in salary schedules and not from movements along existing schedules to higher levels of teacher education and experience. We expect the same was true of the entire decade. Data from the quinquennial survey of NEA members (NEA 1992) indicate that there was little change in the proportion of teachers with master's degrees, at least nationally: 49.3 percent of respondents held master's degrees in 1981, a number that had grown to only 52.6 percent by 1991. Mean years of experience rose from 13 in 1981 to 15 in 1986, where it remained in 1991. Since salary regressions indicate that teachers' pay increases by 2.5 to 3 percent for each additional year of experience, these data suggest that rising levels of work force experience could have raised teacher compensation by 5 to 6 percentage points over this interval (out of a total real increase of 16.5 percent). However, this calculation substantially overstates the portion of salary growth due to changes in experience, since much of the increase in the latter occurred among older career teachers who had already reached the top of their districts' schedules.

Appendix 3C
Ratings of New Teachers

We assume that principals' underlying assessments of their staffs vary continuously. Survey responses are recorded on a five-point scale, however. The mapping from the real line to a five-point scale is determined by the position of the continuous assessment vis-a-vis certain thresholds to be estimated. Thus, an assessment below the lowest threshold results in a rating of "1," whereas a latent assessment above the highest of the thresholds yields a rating of "5." Other ratings correspond to intermediate values. In the first formulation of the model, only state-level salary growth and the ratings given experienced teachers influence the continuous assessment. In the second formulation, the continuous assessment is a function of the other school-level variables examined in table 3.1 as well. By including the ratings given experienced teachers among the explanatory variables, we effectively ask the same question we have asked elsewhere in this chapter: to what extent is the quality of new teachers a function of salary growth, given the quality of experienced teachers. Finally, we assume that the continuous assessment is also a function of a logistically distributed error term. The resulting estimator is known as an ordered logit model, differing from the usual, binary logit in that the dependent variable falls into one of several ordered categories.

We report two sets of estimates below. To interpret the coefficients, note that the probability that new teachers receive a rating below "5" is given by $1/[1+\exp(-Xb-t_4)]$, where Xb is the inner product of the coefficients and the explanatory variables and t_4 is the highest of four thresholds. Hence a negative component of Xb raises the probability of the highest rating, "5." The negative coefficient on relative salary growth therefore indicates that new teachers are more often rated "excellent" in the states that have raised relative salaries the most. The effect is not, however, statistically significant. Other variables behave largely as one would expect. High rates of poverty and concentrations of black and Hispanic students make it more difficult to recruit good teachers, though the effect of poverty is not statistically significant. Location in a large central city or a rural area also impairs recruitment. The starting salary offered teachers with a bachelor's degree and no prior experience has a strong, positive effect on new teacher ratings. This confirms that higher paying districts have an advantage in teacher recruitment, though as we remarked above, these gains come at the expense of other districts.

By substituting different values for salary growth into Xb, it is possible to predict changes in the probability that new teachers receive an excellent rating. The magnitude of the predicted change depends on the other elements of X. To obtain the figure reported in the text, we evaluated all X at their actual values (except for the hypothesized change in salary growth) and averaged the resulting changes in the probability that a rating of "5" was given.

Appendix Table 3C.1 Influence of Salary Growth on Principals' Ratings of New Teachers

	(1)	(2)
Explanatory variables		
Proportional growth in relative teacher salary, 1980-1990	-.449 (.378)	-.428 (.395)
Experienced teachers rated 1	-.083 (1.41)	-.587 (1.20)
Experienced teachers rated 2	1.03 (.249)	.903 (.289)
Experienced teachers rated 3	1.12 (.091)	1.039 (.100)
Experienced teachers rated 4	1.08 (.068)	1.063 (.071)
Starting salary for BA, no experience	---	-.051 (.014)
Proportion of students eligible for free or reduced price lunch	---	.096 (.188)
Proportion of students who are black or Hispanic	---	1.134 (.146)
Location		
Large central city	---	.492 (.120)
Mid-sized central city	---	-.032 (.079)
Rural	---	.393 (.083)
Thresholds		
	-5.425	-4.913
	-3.607	-3.029
	-1.625	-1.038
	.566	1.260
Number of observations	8,249	7,397
-2 Log likelihood	168,034.9	148,166.5

SOURCE: Schools and Staffing Survey, 1990-91. Standard errors in parentheses.

CHAPTER 4

What Went Wrong
Attrition, Vacancies, and the Supply of New Teachers

There is little evidence that higher salaries have raised the quality of newly hired teachers, at least by the indicators of teacher quality we have examined. This calls for an explanation.

One obvious possibility is that teacher labor supply is simply unresponsive to wages. This explanation derives some support from the small percentage of former teachers who cite low pay as their main reason for leaving the position (Choy et al. 1992). Nonetheless, we doubt that the wage elasticity is near zero. Teaching is among the most highly unionized occupations in the United States, a fact that suggests compensation is important to many teachers.[1] Fewer than one-half of the 1987-88 SASS respondents agreed with the statement, "I am satisfied with my salary." Salaries have been found to have a significant effect on teacher attrition (Murnane et al. 1991; Mont and Rees 1996). We present evidence below that salaries also affect the supply of new teachers.

As we will argue in this chapter, the failure of a high-salary policy has its origin in certain key features of the labor market for teachers. These features are the institution of tenure and other forms of job security, the absence of merit pay or other systems for discriminating among teachers when awarding pay raises, costly barriers to entering the profession in the form of certification requirements, and procedures for screening and hiring job applicants that overlook valuable signals of teaching effectiveness. The purpose of this chapter is to describe how these features of the market systematically interact to thwart policy objectives.

Teaching Careers: Preparation, Entry, Tenure

America obtains its public school teachers from the ranks of the college-educated who hold teaching certificates. While certification requirements vary from state to state, as a rule prospective teachers must complete a specified number of credit hours in the subjects for which they seek certification and in pedagogical theory and practice. Prospective teachers are also required to complete a practicum or student teaching experience under the guidance of an established teacher. While the majority of newly certified teachers satisfy these requirements by completing bachelor's degrees in education, this is not the only program of study that leads to certification. College students who major in an academic subject (e.g., history) can meet certification requirements by taking additional courses from a department or school of education. Since the requirements for a major generally exceed the subject-area preparation needed for a certificate, the incremental cost of certification for such individuals is represented by course work in pedagogy (often known as "professional education") and student teaching. There are usually twelve to fifteen semester hours of the former (more for elementary school certification), while student teaching often lasts the better part of a semester.

These are not the only routes into the teaching profession. Persons who have had no undergraduate training in education can become certified in a postgraduate program. Such programs also last a year; many award a master's degree. In recent years, approximately one-ninth of newly certified teachers have come onto the market with master's degrees (Frankel and Stowe 1990). In addition, many states have set up alternative certification routes, typically to facilitate the entry of older persons with work histories outside education. These programs allow such individuals to bypass, or at least postpone, some of the course work associated with certification. Paid internships or other forms of probationary employment generally replace the student teaching practicum. To date these alternative programs have supplied only a small fraction of the nation's newly hired teachers. We discuss them at greater length in the next chapter.[2]

Virtually all states now test teachers. Some tests are a prerequisite for admission to a teacher education program, while others are needed for certification. Many states use tests at both stages. On the whole, passing rates appear to be quite high (80-90 percent), though data are not reported on a consistent basis for all states (Childs and Rudner 1990).

New public school teachers are hired on a probationary status. After a specified period, typically two or three years, teachers who continue to be employed by the same district are granted tenure. While the precise significance of tenure varies with state law and the provisions of collectively bargained contracts, tenure confers important job rights and makes it difficult and expensive for administrators to remove instructors on grounds of incompetence. Other laws and contract provisions also protect more senior teachers against layoffs.

Virtually all public school districts use salary schedules to determine teacher compensation. A schedule is essentially a grid specifying salary as a function of experience and education (degrees or credits). All teachers employed in a district, regardless of grade level or subject matter, are paid on this basis, hence the term, "single salary schedule." Teachers typically reach the top of a district's schedule after fifteen to twenty years' service, though they will continue to receive raises as the entire schedule shifts upward. Teachers who leave one district to take a job in another may or may not be credited in full for prior experience when placed on their new employer's salary schedule; there is considerable variation in local practice here, and it can matter whether the move is within state or across state lines.

Various efforts have been made to change the basis of teacher compensation by introducing performance incentives like merit pay. These reforms have usually been resisted by teacher unions. As a result, merit pay plans tend to be short-lived. Only about 12 percent of public school districts use merit pay, and the amounts at stake appear to be quite small, approximately 2 percent of base pay. (For additional discussion of incentive pay, see chapter 6).

Several features of this career path affect the relationship between salaries and recruitment. First is the single salary schedule, which ensures that when teacher salaries are raised to attract more capable individuals into the profession, all teachers gain.

Second, the institution of tenure and the use of seniority to determine layoffs mean that experienced teachers retain their jobs virtually at will. If higher pay prolongs their careers, there will be fewer job opportunities for newly certified graduates. Note that this is not a purely transitory phenomenon: the steady-state composition of the workforce tilts towards older teachers. There are fewer entry-level jobs in perpetuity.

Third, prospective teachers must invest in an occupation-specific credential that has no market value outside the teaching profession. They must do this before knowing whether they will find a job. As a result, job prospects for new teachers become a relevant consideration when individuals decide whether to undertake teacher training.

Vacancy Rates and the Supply of New Teachers

Figure 4.1 depicts the flow of newly certified teachers onto the labor market between 1976 and 1991, during the years in which the Survey of Recent College Graduates was administered. Flows are measured as a proportion of all new bachelor's degree recipients to control for cyclical fluctuations in the size of the college-age population. Certification rates fell from 1976 through 1981, stabilized in the mid-1980s, and turned up again in the late-1980s. Also shown are the percentage of new graduates employed as full-time public school teachers and the ratio of their salaries to those of other new graduates working full time. Certification rates appear to track employment opportunities more closely than relative pay. Though relative salaries began to rise at the beginning of the 1980s, the percentage of graduates obtaining teaching certificates did not increase until more jobs became available. A cursory inspection of figure 4.1 suggests, then, that employment opportunities are at least as important, and quite possibly more important, than relative salaries in determining the supply of newly certified teachers.

Figure 4.1 also shows that the number of newly certified graduates has exceeded the number hired by public schools in every year of the survey. Although not all newly certified individuals look for teaching jobs, the number of applicants also exceeds the number hired, pointing up an important fact: for all the publicity given to teacher shortages, teacher labor markets typically exhibit excess supply.[3] (There is an excellent discussion of this issue, including the reasons so many forecasts were inaccurate, in Barro 1992.) Because there are fewer vacancies than applicants, prospective teachers are not assured of obtaining a job. The probability of obtaining a job therefore becomes a relevant consideration when deciding whether to invest time and money completing a program of teacher education.

Figure 4.1 Teacher Pay and Entry into Teaching

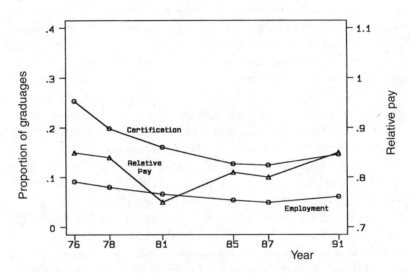

In order to see how large this effect is, we have estimated a probit model of the supply of newly certified graduates as reported by the Surveys of Recent College Graduates. The probability that a graduate has completed a program of teacher education leading to certification is assumed to be a function of job availability, relative salary, and a vector of individual attributes (sex, age, race, marital status, and quality indicators). To measure relative salary, we divide the average salary of new public school teachers by the mean earnings of nonteachers in the same survey cohort. Since state-level means are very noisy, averages are computed for each census region in each survey year. Due to data limitations, region corresponds to the location of the college rather than the graduate's residence or workplace. This ratio may not be the appropriate measure for persons who relocate after completing school, though the fact that the great majority of students remain in the same region suggests that the resulting bias will be slight.[4] Intraregional variation in salaries is also omitted from this measure. Lagged rather than current values enter the model, as the decision to pursue a program of teacher education often predates employment by two years or more.

We expect enrollment in teacher education to fall when jobs are hard to find. Labor market slack is measured as the proportion of applicants who failed to obtain full-time public school positions in the previous wave of the survey. Again, this proportion is calculated at the regional level. Lagged (previous survey) values are used, since prospective teachers must commit themselves to a program of teacher training before the market conditions they will face are revealed.[5] Because this is a regional rather than state-level variable, this measure of job availability raises some of the same concerns as the relative salary variable.

Personal characteristics also influence the decision to teach. Gender, age, and marital status in particular may serve as proxies for unobserved, nonpecuniary returns to teaching. Regional dummies control for further unobserved variation in labor market conditions.

Several variables are introduced as measures of the quality of an applicant's academic background, among them the ranking of the college granting the bachelor's degree and the applicant's undergraduate grade point average. While these variables are intended to capture the influence of academic ability on the decision to teach, it is recognized that they also serve as proxies for personal tastes, since choice of college and the effort made to achieve high grades may well be influenced by career plans. A dummy variable signifying a degree in mathematics and science is also included.

Results are presented in the first column of table 4.1. All variables are statistically significant and have the anticipated signs. Certification probabilities are responsive both to salaries and job availability. The implied elasticities are 2.4 for relative salaries and .74 for job availability. Students with strong academic backgrounds are less likely to complete teacher education.

As noted above, both relative salaries and job availability have been measured imprecisely; while the results clearly indicate that salaries and job availability both matter, the estimated elasticities are only suggestive. In addition, the limited variation in the data (by region and year only) makes it impossible to interact these regressors with measures of teacher quality, a point of some interest, since we would like to know whether persons with stronger academic backgrounds are more sensitive to salaries and job opportunities than others. Unfortunately,

Table 4.1 Influence of Salary and Job Availability on New Teacher Certification

	(1) All survey years	(2) 1991 survey	(3) 1991 survey with quality interactions	(4) 1991 survey, noneducation majors
Relative teacher salary, lagged	1.99 (.18) ***	.379 (.36)	1.42 (2.30)	.92 (.51) *
Job availability, lagged	.75 (.14) ***	1.31 (.98)	7.23 (6.68)	3.39 (1.40) **
College quality:				
Select	-.50 (.03) ***	-.53 (.06) ***	.01 (1.4)	-.19 (.08) **
Above-average	-.28 (.02) ***	-.25 (.05)***	-1.57 (1.14)	-.08 (.06)
Average	-.04 (.02)	-.07 (.04) **	-1.19 (.87)	-.03 (.06)
GPA	.16 (.02) ***	.22 (.04) ***	1.13 (.79)	.11 (.05) **
Math or science degree	-.27 (.03) ***	-.01 (.06)	-1.66 (.128)	.47 (.06) ***
Interactions with salary:				
Select college	-----	-----	-1.41 (1.29)	-----
Above-average college	-----	-----	.44 (.99)	-----
Average college	-----	-----	1.08 (.74)	-----
GPA	-----	-----	.59 (.70)	-----
Math/science degree	-----	-----	2.00 (1.08) *	-----
Interactions with job availability:				
Select college	-----	-----	7.44 (3.43) **	-----
Above-average college	-----	-----	7.75 (2.70) ***	-----
Average college	-----	-----	.33 (2.53)	-----
GPA	-----	-----	2.90 (1.95)	-----
Math/science degree	-----	-----	3.20 (3.47)	-----
Male	-.54 (.02) ***	-.43 (.04) ***	-.43 (.04) ***	-.20 (.05) ***

(continued)

Table 4.1 (continued)

	(1) All survey years	(2) 1991 survey	(3) 1991 survey with quality interactions	(4) 1991 survey, noneducation majors
Married	.31 (.02) ***	.36 (.04) ***	.36 (.04) ***	.17 (.06) ***
Married x male	-.18 (.03) ***	-.20 (.07) ***	-.19 (.07) ***	-.11 (.09)
Hispanic	.13 (.04) ***	.18 (.07) ***	.18 (.07) ***	.27 (.09) ***
Black	.07 (.03) **	-.04 (.06)	-.03 (.06)	.24 (.08) **
Age	-.00 (.00) **	.00 (.00)	.00 (.00)	.00 (.00)
Census regions	yes	yes	yes	yes
Log likelihood	-19,091.66	-4,776.79	-4,756.61	-2,243.31
Number of observations	49,197	12,273	12,273	10,037

SOURCE: Teacher characteristics from Surveys of Recent College Graduates; state average teacher salaries from Digest of Education Statistics; earnings of colleges graduates from 1990 Census; proportion of new teachers from Schools and Staffing Survey, 1987-88.
Significant at 10 percent (*), 5 percent (**), and 1 percent (***).

better measures of job opportunities covering this entire period are not available. Proxies like the growth in enrollment are very imprecise, since demand for new public school teachers is also a function of turnover and the extent to which vacancies are filled by other sources of supply (returning teachers, in-migrants). Data on these determinants of demand are quite incomplete.

However, useful measures of job opportunities are available for the end of the 1980s. The 1987-88 Schools and Staffing Survey furnishes the number of full-time teachers in each school with fewer than three years' experience. Aggregated to the state level, these numbers provide a reasonable measure of demand for the services of new teachers.[6] Since 1990 graduates were deciding on their courses of study at this time, we use these indicators of demand to investigate certification rates for that cohort. To control for differences in state size, job availability is defined as the number of newly hired teachers divided by total public school teacher employment in the state. Relative salary is measured as the average teacher salary divided by the mean earnings of college-educated workers in each state. Other variables are unchanged from column one.

Probit estimates appear in columns two, three and four of table 4.1. In column two, neither salary nor job availability has a statistically significant effect on certification, though the sample size is, of course, much smaller than in column one. The effects of grade point average and college quality are very similar to those reported for the larger sample. In column three we have interacted both salary and job availability with indicators of teacher quality. Most coefficients have large standard errors, a consequence of including so many interaction terms. There are no significant interactions involving salary except for mathematics and science graduates, who are more responsive than the average graduate to an increase in teacher pay, though the effect is only marginally significant. However, a striking pattern emerges with respect to job availability. Graduates of better colleges are much more sensitive than others to market conditions. The implied elasticity for graduates of selective and above average colleges is near unity, though the large standard errors imply that these estimates should be regarded, again, as no more than suggestive.[7]

In the fourth column of table 4.1 we restrict the sample to persons who did not major in education. Members of this group who obtained teacher certification did so while completing an academic major. Among these students, both salary and job availability have a positive and statistically significant influence on the decision to acquire certification. Of the two, job availability has the larger and more important impact.

In summary, an empirical investigation of certification decisions shows that the number of students completing teacher education responds positively to both salaries and job availability, though there is considerable imprecision in our estimates of the magnitude of these effects. In addition, job availability appears to be more important to graduates of better colleges and to students with academic majors, a point to which we return below.

Teacher Attrition and Job Availability

In practice, salaries and job availability are linked. Higher salaries reduce turnover among current staff. As exit from the profession falls, so does the demand for new teachers. Indeed, it did not take long for school systems that raised pay in the 1980s to see feedback from the former to the latter.

> Even the infusion of new teachers, lured to Rochester by the publicized pay increases, was slowed because the high salaries convinced older teachers to defer retirement (*New York Times*, April 10, 1991).

High salaries also jeopardize the job security of new recruits. In Connecticut, where average teacher pay rose 50 percent in real terms during the 1980s, high labor costs compelled many towns to lay off their newest teachers when government revenues fell during the last recession.[8]

As dramatic as such cases are, the impact of salaries on the exit of younger teachers is probably more important. Investigating teachers' career paths in Michigan during the 1970s and 1980s, Richard Murnane and colleagues found that a $4,000 pay raise (in 1988 dollars) reduced the probability that a teacher would quit at the end of the first year by one-third.[9] The percentage of elementary school teachers estimated to teach longer than five years rose from 43 percent to 54 percent. The gain was even greater for high school teachers, from 27 percent to 42 percent. Median career duration among the latter rose nearly two years. While Michigan was in some respects an anomalous case, with many younger persons leaving the state for regions experiencing greater economic growth, estimates for North Carolina teachers confirmed that salaries have a strong effect on the duration of teaching spells. A raise of $4,000 was found to increase median career duration among high school teachers by three and a half years, with the percentage of teachers serving five years or longer advancing from 56 percent to 64 percent.

To illustrate the effect such responses have on the demand for new teachers, we construct a simple model of the composition, by cohorts, of the teaching workforce. A representative career is divided into three segments: an early, seven-year period when exit rates are high, a middle period of twenty-three years when exit rates are low, and a final period of ten years when exit rates again rise. This is a stylized representation of the U-shaped pattern found in empirical studies of teacher attrition (Gilford and Tenenbaum 1990). Baseline values of these exit rates are chosen so that the proportion of teachers in each cohort reflects the actual composition of the U.S. workforce as of the mid-1970s. (First-year teachers are 6 percent of the total; mean work life is fourteen years; etc.) Demand for new teachers is set to 10 percent of each graduating cohort.

We simulate the effect of a pay raise on attrition and new teacher demand under three sets of assumptions:

1. The impact of higher salaries is felt only during the first phase of a career.[10] Annual survival rates are assumed to increase by 3 percent, generating changes in the length of the work life and the five-year survival rate roughly equivalent to the effects of a $4,000 raise on the behavior of Michigan and North Carolina teachers, as described above.

2. Higher salaries affect exit during the mid-career and final career phases as well. We assume an increase of only .5 percent in the one-year survival rate for mid-career teachers. A higher value, 3 percent, is assigned to teachers in the final career phase, reflecting the sizable influence of salary increases on the timing of retirement.

3. One-year survival rates are increased by 5 percent in the first career phase, 1 percent in the middle phase, and 3 percent in the final phase. The implied change in the five-year survival rate remains within the response observed among North Carolina teachers to a $4,000 raise.

A complete description of the construction and calibration of the model is provided in appendix 4A.

Simulated responses are depicted in figure 4.2. Even under our most conservative assumptions, demand for new teachers falls by 10 percent initially, by 15 percent after ten years. When changes in survival rates are larger and more pervasive, as in case three, demand for new teachers falls fully one-third. Note that the changes we have assumed in one-year survival rates are far from extreme. Given that a $4,000 raise represents only 12 percent of the average 1988 salary in Michigan and 16 percent of the mean salary in North Carolina, it is likely that even our third simulation underestimates the response to salary increases of 20 percent or more in "high-growth" states.

Figure 4.2 Demand for New Teachers, Following a Salary Increase

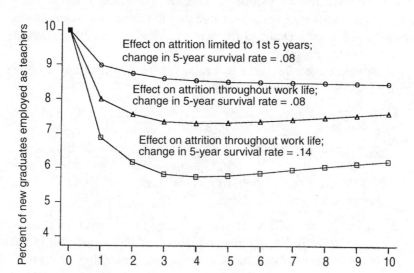

Screening and the Quality of Teacher Applicants

Figure 4.2 shows how an increase in teacher salaries feeds back on the demand for new teachers. Since the supply of new teachers is sensitive to job availability, this feedback dampens their response to higher pay. This analysis does not establish, of course, that raising salaries does no good. Indeed, with fewer jobs to fill, school districts can be more selective in their hiring decisions. A pay increase should constitute, at worst, a mixed blessing: new teachers of better quality, albeit fewer of them.

This argument supposes that more capable individuals will continue to apply despite declining demand for teachers.[11] Given the opportunity cost of their investment in teacher education, however, these persons are more likely than the average applicant to pursue an alternative career when their job prospects deteriorate. Much depends, then, on the way job applicants are screened. If the market fails to show preference to better candidates for the jobs that remain, their share of the applicant pool may fall.

Previous investigations of teachers' entry into the labor market have provided little systematic information about the way job candidates are screened. While it has been recognized that newly certified teachers with the highest test scores and the strongest academic records are less likely to enter the teaching corps, this phenomenon is generally explained as a consequence of individual choice: "Presumably, the most able could have obtained teaching jobs" (Nelson 1985).[12] Information that would permit a test of this conjecture—the identity of persons who actually sought teaching positions—has been missing from the data sets most often used to investigate the career paths of new teachers.[13]

This is not the case in the Surveys of Recent College Graduates, which identify job applicants. Figure 4.3 displays certification, application and entry rates among new bachelor's degree recipients by college quality. These data exhibit the pattern found in other studies: the higher the quality of the undergraduate institution, the less likely a student is to enter a teaching career. This is partly due to differences in application rates: 75 percent of the certified graduates of selective and above-average schools seek teaching positions, compared to 85 percent elsewhere. A larger share of better educated students select out of the applicant pool at this stage. However, as figure 4.3 also shows, this pattern is not reversed at the next stage, when applicants are screened for the available positions. *Applicants from more selective colleges do not fare better in the job market; indeed, remarkably, they do somewhat worse.* This pattern also characterizes data disaggregated by survey years and by region.

If teacher candidates from better colleges are no more successful than graduates of the least selective colleges, the offsetting effects described above come into full play. The more capable applicants, who would be attracted to teaching by higher salaries, are at the same time discouraged by the reduction in job openings. The poorer their chances of obtaining a job, the more likely the second effect is to cancel the first. The net result: little change in the applicant mix and little improvement in the quality of new recruits.

Evidence presented earlier shows that this is not a remote theoretical possibility. As reported in table 4.1, certification decisions are more sensitive to job availability, the better the college attended. It is difficult to explain why this should be so, unless these graduates felt the effects of a declining job market. Still, the evidence examined so far is not wholly persuasive. A variety of confounding factors might obscure the positive effect that college quality has on job prospects within teaching. Since this point is central to our argument, we devote the remainder of this section to it.

To begin, not all applicants are equally serious about teaching. For some a teaching job may represent a fallback option should a preferred job fail to materialize. This may be especially true of applicants from better colleges. To assess the importance of this phenomenon, we adjust the figures on job applicants by excluding all persons whose subsequent activities suggest they may have turned down teaching jobs (among them, all full-time students). Remaining applicants either obtained a full-time public school position or gave evidence of an unsuccessful search in one of the following ways:

1. By working part time despite expressing a preference for full-time work

2. By taking a teaching job in a private school[14]

Figure 4.3 Entry of New Teachers, by College Rank

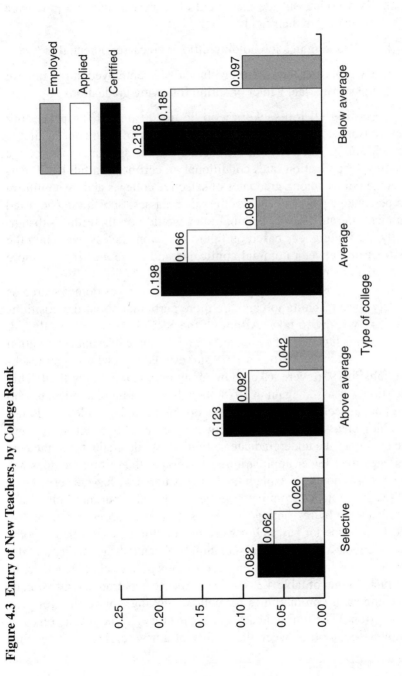

3. By working outside their field of study because "no jobs were available" in their fields

4. By working in a job holding little or no career potential

5. By reporting they were involuntarily unemployed at the time of the survey (late winter or spring following graduation)

Excluding all job seekers who do not fit one of the preceding descriptions considerably reduces the number of graduates available for a teaching job; however, the decline is quite similar across college rankings. Application rates conditional on certification fall by 20 percentage points among graduates of selective colleges and by a uniform 15 percentage points in each of the other classes. Substituting adjusted application rates for the original rates would not, therefore, substantially alter inferences based on figure 4.3. Nonetheless, we retain the distinction between nominal applicants and those meeting the more restrictive definition for use in further analysis.

It is also possible that graduates of better colleges do not search as widely for a teaching job and are more particular about the positions they are willing to take. Although the SRCG do not generally ask respondents how hard they looked for a job, some relevant information was reported in the 1976 and 1978 surveys. Persons who sought teaching jobs in 1976 were asked how many applications they filed. This question was asked again in 1978, though only of those applicants who did not subsequently teach. The results, presented in table 4.2, do not exhibit a clear-cut relationship between the intensity of job search and the quality of the undergraduate institution. While graduates of the best colleges filed fewer applications on average, the difference does not seem large enough to explain the hiring patterns we have observed.

Teacher trainees from better colleges may also put themselves at a disadvantage by restricting their job search to a subset of school districts with superior pay and/or working conditions. To test this hypothesis, we look for a positive association between college quality and the pay and working conditions enjoyed by new public school teachers. In the first column of table 4.3, we report coefficients from a regression of teaching salary on dummies for college ranking, controlling for year and region. (The omitted category is "average.") The results reveal a slight association between the quality of a new teacher's college and that teacher's earnings. (The difference between select and below-average is significant at 10 percent. However, these differences amount to only a few hundred dollars. When we allow for the fact that teachers from better colleges are more likely to work in metropolitan areas, where costs of living are higher, the gap seems trivial. There is little support here for the notion that teachers from better colleges have, as a group, held out for jobs offering substantially higher pay.

Table 4.2. Application Rates by College Ranking

College ranking	Number of applications	
	1976	1978[a]
Selective	11.7	16.1
Above-average	14.3	14.1
Average	16.6	19.5
Below-average	12.2	19.4
Number of observations	1,804	444

SOURCE: Surveys of Recent College Graduates, 1976 and 1978.
a. Question was asked only of applicants who did not subsequently teach.

Since the SRCG do not obtain information on working conditions, we turn to the Schools and Staffing Survey of 1987-88 for evidence on teaching environments.[15] As shown in columns two and three of table 4.3, graduates of better colleges tend to work in schools with smaller percentages of poor students and higher percentages of students bound for college. However, the differences by college quality are small, particularly among the top three rankings.

The poverty rate is a proxy for behavioral and learning problems found more often among low socioeconomic status students. The Schools and Staffing Survey also asked teachers for a direct assessment of the severity of the following problems: physical and verbal abuse of teachers, fighting, pregnancies, vandalism, and the carrying of weapons to school. For each of these items, we constructed two measures of severity, the first indicating that the teacher regarded it as a serious problem in the school, the second that it was judged a moderate problem. The Mantel-Haenszel chi-square statistic was computed to measure the association between college background and the perceived severity of each problem. In only three cases—the perception of physical abuse of teachers, verbal abuse of teachers, and vandalism as moderately severe problems within the school—did this statistic exceed the 10 percent level of significance. Moreover, the association was in the wrong direction, i.e., teachers from better colleges were *more* likely to work in schools in which they found these problems moderately severe. This is likely due to the fact that more of these graduates work in large cities.

Table 4.3. Teaching Pay, Working Conditions by College Ranking

College ranking	Teaching pay[a]	Student poverty rate[b] Mean (Std. dev.)	No. of obs.	College application rate[c] Mean (Std. dev.)	No. of obs.
Selective	298 (271)	.286 (.271)	257	.532 (.225)	116
Above-average	71 (140)	.281 (.251)	617	.532 (.219)	229
Average	----	.301 (.260)	1,945	.515 (.213)	745
Below-average	-200 (124)	.354 (.217)	1,163	.502 (.218)	457
No. of jobs.	5,208	----	3,182	----	1,547

SOURCES: Surveys of Recent College Graduates; Schools and Staffing Survey 1987-88.
a. Teaching pay coefficients obtained from regression of full–time public school teaching salary on college ranking, regional and year dummies. Standard errors in parentheses, corrected for heteroscedasticity.
b. Student poverty rate = proportion of students eligible for free or reduced–price lunch.
c. College application rate = proportion of graduating seniors applying to college. Calculated for secondary schools only.

In conclusion, we find virtually no evidence to support the claim that graduates of better colleges do not find teaching jobs because they are less willing than others to accept low pay and difficult working conditions. Still, it is possible that other confounding factors obscure the relationship between college quality and labor market outcomes. To assess this hypothesis, we regress the probability that an applicant obtains a full-time public school teaching position on a set of labor market conditions and personal characteristics. The latter include aspects of the candidate's academic background and professional preparation—grade point average, certification fields, college quality, major subject—as well as demographic variables that may influence a hiring decision—age, gender, marital status, race, and ethnicity. Two additional variables indicate how much time an individual has had to obtain a job. The first is the number of months that have elapsed since graduation, the second a binary variable indicating that the applicant did not receive a teaching certificate until after graduation.

Since the probability that an applicant will receive an offer depends greatly on the need for new public school teachers, we include various indicators of demand. Our first measure is the ratio of newly hired teachers to the size of the graduating cohort. Because there are too few observations to obtain accurate state-level values, this variable is constructed as the ratio of regional aggregates. We also use, in place of this measure, a set of regional and survey year fixed effects. Finally, we estimate a model containing a full set of state and year interactions, allowing demand to vary by state and by year.

The sample is limited to persons who meet the more stringent (adjusted) definition of applicant given above; however, quite similar results obtain when the sample is based on the original, unadjusted definition of a teaching applicant.[16]

The first two variants of the model were estimated by probit. Results were so similar that we report only the first variant in table 4.4 (column one). The third variant was estimated as a linear probability model due to the large number of state by year effects (column two). Since the coefficients of the linear model are easier to interpret and support the same conclusions as those in column one, our discussion focuses on them.

The introduction of background controls has, if anything, strengthened our earlier conclusion. Not only does college quality fail to improve an applicant's job prospects, there is evidence, albeit marginally significant, that graduates of above average and average colleges fare worse on the job market than graduates of below-average schools (the omitted category).

Results are only slightly more encouraging with respect to other aspects of academic background. A degree in mathematics or science raises an applicant's prospects of success by 8 to 9 percent (the sum of the coefficients on a math or science major and math or science certification, statistically significant at 10 percent). However, the effect of a bachelor's degree in education is equally strong, a disconcerting finding, given efforts to recruit more teachers with subject area majors.

Table 4.4. Influence of Teacher Attributes on Job Offers

Explanatory variables	(1) Probit estimates	(2) Linear probability estimates[a]
College rank		
Selective	.053	.018
	(.118)	(.035)
Above-average	−.059	−.042*
	(.081)	(.025)
Average	−.046	−.034*
	(.062)	(.019)
Below-average	---	---
Undergraduate GPA	.284***	.106***
	(.060)	(.015)
Degree in math or science	.238	.064
	(.159)	(.048)
Degree in education	.250***	.087***
	(.094)	(.027)
Certification areas		
Early childhood	−.057	−.027
	(.061)	(.016)
Elementary	.085	.029
	(.096)	(.028)
Special education	.418***	.147***
	(.072)	(.016)
Math or science	.064	.021
	(.083)	(.020)
Elementary or early childhood certification		
x education degree	−.036	−.011
	(.096)	(.032)
Month since graduation	.016**	.005***
	(.007)	(.002)
Certification received after graduation	−.256***	−.097***
	(.068)	(.018)
Teacher characteristics		
Male	.090	.040***
	(.078)	(.020)
Married	−.074	−.026**
	(.061)	(.015)

Table 4.4 (continued)

Explanatory variables	(1) Probit estimates	(2) Linear probability estimates[a]
Married male	.286**	.090***
	(.120)	(.032)
Age	−.001	−.001
	(.004)	(.001)
Hispanic	.542***	.128***
	(.161)	(.029)
Black	−.034	.001
	(.104)	(.027)
Market demand		
Region (omitted west)		
NE	−.511***	---
	(.096)	
NC	−.436***	---
	(.089)	
South	−.162	---
	(.109)	
Newly hired teachers as share of all graduates	7.03***	---
	(1.97)	
State, year, and state x year interactions	no	yes
Intercept	−1.24***	−.012
	(.153)	(.007)
Number of observations	8,940	8,940
Log likelihood / R^2	−1740.99	.14

SOURCE: Surveys of Recent college Graduates.
a. Standard errors corrected for heteroscedasticity.

Since the model includes an interaction between education majors and persons with certificates in early childhood and elementary education, this coefficient applies specifically to applicants for secondary school positions. The implication is that an individual who wishes to teach mathematics or science at the secondary school level is better off majoring in education with a teaching field in math or science than completing an academic major in one of those disciplines. Of the variables measuring the quality of an applicant's academic record, only grade point average has a significant, positive impact on the probability of a successful job search. It is somewhat curious that school districts care about grades but not about the quality of the institution or academic program awarding them, an indication that grades may matter as much for the information they contain about an applicant's affective characteristics (e.g., diligence) as for the signal they furnish of cognitive ability.[17]

Recapitulation: Critical Features of the Labor Market

In the introduction to this chapter, we listed several features of the teacher labor market that interact in ways that undermine the attainment of policy objectives. We now restate the argument of the preceding pages to highlight their role.

One would expect an industry that raises wages to improve the quality of the workers it recruits in two ways. First, the number of applicants rises. Even if there is no change in the average ability of those applicants, the mere fact that there are more of them permits employers to be more discriminating about those they hire. In addition, the quality of the applicant pool improves. The marginal applicants who are attracted by higher salaries are persons whose reservation wages exceeded the pay formerly offered by the industry. Unless the skills required by this industry are wholly idiosyncratic, it is to be expected that persons who command higher salaries elsewhere will, on average, perform more capably in this sector as well. Thus there are two channels by which the ability of the workforce rises: one, an increase in the number of applicants relative to vacancies, allowing employers to raise the standards job applicants must meet; and two, an influx of more capable applicants at the margin, raising the quality of the applicant pool. Under these conditions, it would seem next to impossible for a salary increase to fail of its purpose.

However, as we have already seen, this argument overlooks some important features of the teacher labor market. First, *public schools pay teachers on the basis of their experience and their academic credentials—not on the basis of their teaching performance.* Pay increases are not targeted to the type of persons one wants to attract into teaching but are delivered across the board. As a result, more older workers decide to stay on, vacancy rates fall, and the demand for new teachers declines. Indeed, our calculations indicate that pay raises on the order of 20 percent could easily diminish the demand for new teachers by one-third. Nor is it possible to circumvent these consequences by removing the worst of the older teachers from their jobs—*tenure and other forms of job security* close this option.

The decline in demand for new teachers will clearly delay any improvement in the workforce. But the problems are not merely transitional. The decline in job openings feeds back on the quality of applicants, since *it is costly to enter the applicant pool.* Prospective public school teachers are required to spend time and effort acquiring a license to teach before knowing whether they will have a job. Since this license is of no value outside the occupation, application rates become a function of job availability as well as wages. In recent years, teacher labor markets have been characterized by excess supply. This situation is exacerbated when salaries rise, for the number of job openings declines at the same time the number of job seekers rises. The effect of excess supply is not neutral when it comes to teacher quality: the better an individual's options outside teaching, the more costly the investment in a teaching credential if, in fact, no job materializes. Thus, persons with attractive options will be less likely to enter the applicant pool as job opportunities disappear, just as they were more likely to enter the pool when salary increases made teaching more competitive with other occupations. Whether they enroll in programs of teacher education depends critically on how confident they remain of their own job prospects in a declining market. The evidence examined above suggests they do not feel very confident, and with good reason. *Applicants from better colleges, as well as graduates of more rigorous programs of study, have no discernible advantage in the market for public school positions.* As a result, the decline in job openings poses a significant deterrent to prospective teachers with attractive outside options.

It is unlikely that this deterrent fully offsets the incentive created by higher salaries in the first place. On the contrary, there will probably be more applicants for teaching positions. But—and this is the key point—there will be more applicants of every type. Since persons with attractive options outside teaching are more responsive both to the incentive and to the deterrent, their share of the applicant pool is not likely to increase very much. Indeed, under plausible assumptions it declines, as we show in appendix 4C.

Even this might not matter greatly if school systems concentrated on hiring the best of those who apply: after all, the need for new teachers has diminished; districts can be more selective. But districts do not appear to select on the basis of the indicators of quality we have used. Indeed, if they did, high-quality applicants need not have been discouraged in the first place. The result: with no improvement in the applicant pool, and no marked tendency on the part of districts to select on the basis of our indicators of quality, there is little or no improvement in the qualifications of new teachers.

Responses to Skeptics

At this point a skeptic might interrupt as follows: "Your results merely demonstrate that school officials do not agree with the National Commission on Excellence in Education and other blue-ribbon task forces about the criteria to be used in screening teacher applicants. The commissions thought it was of great importance to hire teachers with stronger academic records; educational practitioners apparently think otherwise. The fact that school officials do not give much weight to these criteria when deciding whom to hire only shows that you have been looking at the wrong set of characteristics, not that raising pay has failed to improve the workforce."

However, the mere fact that school districts are not using our indicators of quality does not mean the indicators are valueless. It may be, instead, that the practices of school officials need to change. As noted in chapter 2, significant positive relationships have been shown between these indicators of teacher quality and student achievement. Recall, too, that by principals' own ratings of their new teachers, higher salaries do not appear to have contributed very much to the quality of the workforce. Principals in states that have raised pay the most are only slightly more positive about the new teachers they have recruited than are principals elsewhere. This finding poses questions about the value of the information used to make personnel decisions.

Unfortunately, little is known about the way school districts screen job applicants. Scholarly research takes the form of case studies and provides scarcely more than anecdotal evidence (Murnane et al. 1991; Gilford and Tenenbaum 1990; Wise et al., 1987). Yet what we know does not inspire confidence. So far as we can tell, applicants for teaching positions are not generally asked to teach a class as part of the interview process. Some research suggests that school recruiters give too much weight to the impression an applicant makes during a job interview, too little to a record of academic achievement assembled over a period of many years. Webster's (1988) study of hiring and teacher evaluation in the Dallas school system showed that teachers' scores on tests of verbal and quantitative ability were the best predictors of student achievement test gains; however, interviews and personal references were more important than test scores and transcripts in determining who was hired. Likewise, a telephone poll of large urban school systems conducted for the Dallas schools and cited in the same study found that interviews generally carried the most weight in the selection of teachers. Results were more negative yet in Perry's (1981) examination of labor market entry for a small sample of teacher training graduates in Texas: among those who sought teaching jobs, there were no significant differences between successful and unsuccessful candidates with respect to grade point averages, student teaching evaluations, and recommendations.

It could be argued that schools currently overlook applicants with strong academic records, if such individuals show less promise for other reasons. One liability is sufficiently well documented to merit further discussion. As noted in chapter 3, individuals with strong academic backgrounds are more likely to leave teaching within a few years. Teachers' quit rates are positively related to scores on the SAT and the NTE (Schlechty and Vance 1981; Murnane and Olsen 1990) and to college quality (Ballou and Podgursky 1993a). Thus, on this argument, school officials are right to reject candidates with stronger academic backgrounds, given the costs of high turnover.

Two propositions need to be distinguished here. The first is that school officials turn down applicants who are more likely to quit. We do not doubt that this is factually correct. Whether they have arrived at the optimal trade-off between turnover and quality is another question. A few calculations based on a simple model of the makeup of the teaching workforce suggest that current practices are far from optimal. (Details are presented in appendix 4B.)

To keep the analysis simple, we suppose there are two types of teachers, low quality and high quality. Given the same level of experience, the latter make better teachers. However, they also exhibit higher rates of attrition. Assumptions about quit behavior are based on the studies of teacher attrition cited above. Seven-year survival rates among the low-quality teachers are assumed to range between 50 and 60 percent. High-quality teachers are one-half to two-thirds as likely to last this long. In addition, we assume that teachers reach full effectiveness after four years, as research on education production functions indicates that virtually all the gains from experience accrue in the first few years (Hanushek 1981). Finally, new teachers are assumed to be only half as effective as they eventually become. Solving the model for mean teaching effectiveness reveals that preference should be given to low-quality applicants only if they are at least 96 percent as effective as a high-quality applicant with the same experience.

This result is highly robust to reasonable changes in the model's parameters. Lengthening the period during which teachers learn on the job to seven years lowers the critical ratio by only 5 percentage points, from 96 percent to 91 percent. Similarly, even if beginning teachers are only one-fifth as effective as they later become (thus raising the value of experience), it is optimal to prefer low-quality teachers only if they are at least 91 percent as effective as applicants of higher quality. Varying turnover rates makes little difference, provided the implied difference in survivor functions remains within the bounds that have been reported in the literature.

We conclude that while school officials may be motivated by the desire to hold down turnover, it is exceedingly difficult to defend hiring practices that give preference to individuals of less initial ability on these grounds. These are not, of course, the only costs associated with turnover. Since the mean spell length for teachers of low quality (under our assumptions) falls between 16 and 18 years, while the mean spell for high quality teachers lies between 7 and 9 years, keeping a position staffed with a high-quality teacher will require recruiting almost twice as often. However, the expected difference—the cost of filling a position once every 7-9 years instead of once every 16-18 years—appears to be no more than a trivial addition to the costs schools routinely incur in order to deal with turnover. It should also be noted that this analysis has assumed that once teachers hit their stride, their teaching never deteriorates thereafter. A more realistic assumption would, of course, reduce the bias that presently favors low-attrition, low-quality instructors, making it even harder to defend current practices.

In conclusion, it is very difficult to make the case for the optimality of current hiring practices on the basis of differential turnover rates. On the contrary, recruiting persons who might teach for a few years (as opposed to a long career) represents one of the most promising ways to raise the quality of the workforce.

> In a society with abundant opportunities for talented college graduates and a tradition of labor market mobility, it will never be possible to persuade two million of them to teach their whole lives. Public rhetoric that implies personal failure when a teacher leaves the classroom after successfully teaching for a number of years may deter many of them from ever setting foot in a classroom (Murnane et al. 1991).

This does not, of course, exhaust the objections schools might have to hiring teachers with strong academic records. Rather than attempt to anticipate all such arguments, let us suppose that these officials are right. Suppose, then, that the criteria we have been using bear little relationship to teaching effectiveness, and that they are rightly disregarded by districts when new teachers are hired. Presumably there are some other criteria that districts use to assess candidates.[18] One of two things must be true. Either these criteria are idiosyncratic to teaching (so that persons who fare well by these measures do not have superior alternatives outside teaching), or at least some of the characteristics and traits that make a good teacher enhance one's marketability in other careers. The first of these alternatives is not very plausible; moreover, if true, it substantially weakens the case for raising teacher salaries. Higher pay will increase the number of applicants, but not their quality—indeed, quality may fall, if the idiosyncratic qualities that make good teachers (e.g., love of children) are associated with low reservation wages. If these qualities are also hard to observe ex ante, as seems likely given they are unrelated to signals of productivity in other occupations, an increase in the number of applicants that does not raise mean quality leaves schools hiring essentially the same kind of teachers as before.

Consider, then, the second alternative, implying that good teachers must be bid away from other occupations. Everything we have said about graduates with strong academic records remains true of this group. In particular, persons with better options outside teaching are more likely to be deterred by a declining demand for new teachers, since they will have paid a higher opportunity cost if no job is forthcoming. They will overlook the general decline in job openings only if they can be confident that their own job prospects remain good. Yet what grounds can they have for this belief? Note that we are discussing a career decision on the part of college undergraduates. If good grades and high test scores do not matter, what indicators of their own employability will they possess? At the point where the decision must be made, these individuals will have little else to go on when attempting to assess their chances on the teacher job market. They will not yet have done any student teaching. They will have had no opportunity to show instructors in their professional education courses that they possess the commitment, enthusiasm, imagination, etc., that will make them good teachers. If one's academic record is irrelevant, it becomes very difficult to assess with any accuracy one's chances on the job market. This is not to say that only accurate assessments matter. Indeed, it may be that those who enroll in teacher education are, on the whole, overly optimistic. But excessive optimism would presumably affect all types of potential candidates—it is not a mechanism on which we can rely to select into the applicant pool those who will make the best teachers.

To this point we have considered arguments that might be raised by a reader who accepts our analysis of the teacher labor market but denies that there is anything much to worry about in the way this market functions. We now turn to a different kind of objection, namely, that the features of the labor market that we have deemed important cannot represent more than minor hindrances to efforts to recruit better teachers. This argument derives some plausibility from the observation that nothing in our analysis would seem to pertain uniquely to teacher labor markets. In all professions, an increase in salary will reduce exit rates, leading to a drop in demand for new recruits. Other professions, too, have their licensing requirements, many of them involving much more professional education than teaching. Are we arguing for the implausible proposition that no professional workforce can be improved by an increase in its compensation? Or have we exaggerated the importance of these factors?

In fact, there are some critical differences between teaching and other professions. These differences have a substantial effect on the opportunity costs of professional training and the deterrent posed by a decline in job openings.

Professions like medicine, law, and accounting offer a broad range of employment opportunities. At one end are the most prestigious hospitals, clinics, and firms offering large salaries and prospects of organizational advancement. At the other end are small entrepreneurs in private practice. When the supply of new professionals rises relative to demand on the part of established firms, the overflow enters private practice where conditions are quite competitive. For this very reason it is difficult to conceive of circumstances that would produce an across-the-board increase in incomes together with rising excess supply. If the best-established firms (hospitals, etc.) offer higher pay in conditions of stable demand, the resulting increase in supply will drive down incomes in private practice, which will in turn moderate the supply response.

In addition, we are aware of no other profession where compensation and contract renewal are so largely divorced from evaluations of performance as they are in public school teaching. In most cases, when new recruits enter the employ of established firms, they face extended probationary periods when their performance is carefully monitored. Young lawyers at large law firms face highly competitive "up or out" tournaments in promotion to partner. In other professions, such as dentistry and veterinary medicine, pay and advancement within the organization are explicitly tied to individual or small group performance. More generally, the use of performance incentives is widespread throughout the corporate sector (Milkovich and Newman 1993). Pay flexibility implies, of course, that efforts to improve the workforce need not involve across-the-board raises.[19]

Since the least successful job seekers can enter private practice, an investment in professional training is rarely a complete waste. One can generally earn a living practicing one's profession, though perhaps not on the scale one hoped for. Matters are quite different in teaching. If a newly certified teacher does not obtain a public school job, the investment in acquiring certification is basically wasted. There is virtually no private practice. There are a limited number of positions in private schools and in tutoring services (e.g., Sylvan Learning Centers), though not enough to absorb all unsuccessful applicants for public school jobs. More important, few of these alternative employment opportunities require a license. In general, state certification is not needed to teach in the private sector, nor is it of much help in securing a teaching job. Even those private schools that nominally require their teachers to be certified often allow them to earn this license after they have begun working. Thus, the incentive to undertake an up-front investment in a teaching license depends critically on the availability of public school jobs and little else.

Finally, teaching differs significantly from other professions in that the quality of one's academic record plays a major role in determining access to the best programs of professional education and the best jobs. Candidates from the most selective schools (and the top of the class at these same schools) unquestionably fare better in the market. Rankings of the programs are well known in the profession and guide recruitment. Jobs at the most prestigious law firms, hospitals, or corporations tend to go to the graduates of the top programs, where admissions are based, in turn, on undergraduate records and examination scores. Compared to students considering teaching careers, those contemplating careers in law, medicine, accounting, etc. are far better able to assess their chances of obtaining a high-paid position. As a result, even if high salaries create an excess number of applicants, clear signals are sent to the best candidates that their services are still in demand.

Still, it may be that we have attached too much importance to these factors. Yes, higher salaries may make it harder for new graduates to find a job. But is it that difficult or costly to obtain a teaching certificate? Implicit in our analysis must be some implausible assumptions—perhaps that prospective teachers are unusually risk averse, or that they overestimate the decline in job openings (a mistake that would, presumably, right itself with time).

It is difficult to respond to this objection, as the empirical literature provides few reliable estimates of key determinants of teacher supply. There is virtually no research on the importance of job availability; indeed, it is common to find market-clearing assumptions in both theoretical and empirical models (e.g., Manski 1987; Zarkin 1985). Yet according to the estimates in table 4.1, demand for new teachers is an important determinant of certification rates. Indeed, interactions of job availability with college quality and academic major were more important than interactions of the same indicators with pay. If these estimates are taken at face value, they support the conclusion that higher pay will lower overall applicant quality: larger salaries attract more applicants of every type (roughly in proportion to their original shares of the pool), while declining job opportunities selectively screen out the best.

Yet the estimates in table 4.1 are not very precise. Most of them are based on a single cross-section from 1990. Rather than rest the full weight of the analysis on these findings, in appendix 4C we present an alternative examination of the relationship between salaries, job availability, and the career decisions of prospective teachers. The model we employ assumes risk-neutral agents with perfect knowledge of salaries and the probability of obtaining a teaching job—thus prospective teachers are not overreacting in either sense mentioned above. There are two kinds of teachers: high ability and low ability. The decision to pursue a teaching career is based on a comparison of the income derived from teaching (including nonpecuniary benefits) with the income available from one's best alternative choice. Thanks to the structure of the model, elasticities of dubious accuracy are not required to evaluate the effect of raising teacher pay; rather, the data required are average length of teaching careers, earnings outside education, and the opportunity cost and out-of-pocket expense of teacher training. Some assumptions must be made about unobservables, notably the nonpecuniary returns to teaching. However, extreme assumptions are not required to generate our central finding, that higher salaries can fail to produce any improvement in teacher recruitment.

Finally, we return to the possibility that salaries have simply not increased enough. If teacher supply is not very responsive to salary, or if teachers are skeptical that wage gains will be preserved, increases in pay must be larger and more lasting to have a significant impact on teacher quality.

As we have noted, there is considerable uncertainty about the magnitude of salary elasticities, given the lack of reliable data on teacher supply. Consider, however, the case of Connecticut, where teacher salaries rose 50 percent in real terms between 1980 and 1990. Connecticut teachers are now the highest paid in the nation, earning an average salary of $48,850 in 1992-93. The policy pursued by Connecticut probably represents the upper bound on what is politically feasible with respect to teacher pay. Those who continue to call for higher salaries for teachers can scarcely expect that other states will do more than this.

The result has been a glut of teachers on the market. In the 1992-93 school year Connecticut districts received 559 applications *for each* elementary school vacancy. There is excess supply even in such traditionally hard-to-fill subjects as math and science. In the same school year, districts received 40 applications per vacancy in biology or general science, 13 for each vacancy in earth or physical sciences. Between 50 and 100 applications were received for every opening at the secondary level in humanities, social science, arts, and mathematics (Beaudin 1994-95). While many candidates filed multiple applications, this behavior does not explain away these ratios. A 1993 survey of newly trained teachers who succeeded in obtaining public school employment found that half had submitted seven or fewer applications. The modal response was one, and only 2.6 percent of the respondents blanketed the state. Many of these individuals worked as substitute teachers, teacher's aides, or part-time teachers. Indeed, these appear to be the most important avenues into public school employment; nearly three-quarters of these teachers indicated they found their current positions through personal networking (substitute or student teaching, direct contact with the district, information from a colleague or friend) as opposed to advertisements or placement bulletins.

There can be no doubt that this kind of labor market is discouraging to prospective teachers.[20] When newly trained teachers must take low-paid, low-status jobs as aides or substitutes, when personal contacts ("who you know") become the most important means for obtaining a public school position, talented individuals with attractive outside options are likely to continue to pass up teaching in favor of alternative careers.

Conclusion

In chapter 3 we concluded that the salary increases awarded teachers in the 1980s have done little to improve the workforce. In this chapter we have looked at the workings of the teacher labor market in an effort to understand why this policy misfired. Several factors seem to be responsible, among them an exacerbation of excess supply, resulting in declining job opportunities for new teachers and an increased likelihood that an investment in teacher training would be wasted. The last factor is not neutral when it comes to teacher quality: the better an individual's options outside teaching, the more costly the mistake if no job materializes.

All this might not matter very much if the market signaled the best prospective teachers that their services remain in demand. This does not appear to occur. On the contrary, when hiring new teachers, school districts appear to place little or no weight on measures of academic achievement and cognitive ability that are valued in other professions.

Several years ago John Chubb and Eric Hanushek anticipated this discussion in their essay for the Brookings publication, *Setting National Priorities*:

> Some analysts argue, for example, that higher salaries will improve the pool of teachers. This argument, with which few would disagree, does not, however, establish that the quality of teaching will improve, because it is still necessary to select and to retain the better people from any enlarged pool. The research on performance indicates that schools have not developed effective salary policies. The exact mechanism leading to this result is not really known; it could be poor selection, poor promotion, or poor retention. But the outcome is clear (Chubb and Hanushek 1990).

While we would agree with the conclusion of these authors, we believe the reasons for policy failure have been more obscure than they suppose. Precisely because selection is poor and because tenured teachers are more likely to remain in their jobs when salaries rise, there is no assurance that even the first objective of salary reform can be achieved, namely an improvement in the ability of those who seek to become teachers.

NOTES

1. In 1988, 19 percent of the U.S. workforce was unionized. The share of public sector employees was 43 percent. Among public school teachers it was 75 percent (Corme, Hirsch, and MacPherson 1990).

2. There is also an irregular route into teaching, as virtually all states allow districts facing a shortage of applicants to hire uncertified teachers on an emergency basis. Continued employment is contingent on completion of conventional licensing requirements within a set period of time. According to the 1990-91 Schools and Staffing Survey, fewer than 5 percent of new teachers are hired on these terms. It is impossible to be more precise, since the item on the SASS refers to teachers hired on a "provisional" basis. In many states, new teachers certified through traditional routes are considered to have "provisional" certificates, with a "standard" certificate awarded after the completion of a certain number of years of service and, in some states, additional education. This inconsistent terminology may well have resulted in some misclassification of new teachers. Since the error would have been one-sided, it seems safe to conclude that the proportion of new teachers with emergency certificates could have been no greater than 5 percent.

3. Although the fact that the aggregate number of applicants exceeds total vacancies does not imply an absence of shortages, since some areas may have too many applicants while others have too few, there is little evidence that shortages occur to any significant extent. The 1990-91 Schools and Staffing Survey reports that qualified candidates were found for more than 99 percent of all public school teaching positions.

4. The SRCG provide the location of college and workplace in only one-half of the survey years. When both are available, data indicate that approximately 90 percent of teachers work within the same region in which they attend college. As one would expect, the proportion is smaller for graduates of selective colleges, though still over 80 percent.

5. One might think that market conditions at the time of graduation would also matter; however, the costs of pursuing a teaching job at this stage (mailing out resumes, going to interviews) are considerably smaller than those associated with the investment in training. In fact, they do not appear to deter applicants even when job prospects are poor. In their responses to the SRCGs, a negligible proportion of newly certified graduates indicated that they declined to apply for a teaching job for the reason that "jobs are hard to find."

6. This would not be true had new teacher markets been supply-constrained. However, given that teacher labor markets have generally been in a state of excess supply, the numbers of new teachers hired represent demand.

A longer series is not available. Published data provide only the aggregate number of teachers, not the number newly hired. Since most of the demand for new teachers is replacement demand, trends in aggregate employment can provide a highly misleading picture of the job market for new teachers.

7. Additional variants of the model (not reported here) included controls for working conditions (weighted averages of the characteristics of the communities and schools where new teachers had been hired) and alternative measures of salary (e.g., beginning teacher pay rather than mean salary). Neither specification changed the central finding on the interactions of job availability and college quality.

8. "The [Connecticut] Educational Enhancement Act . . . is widely identified with higher teacher salaries. . . . Because retirement benefits are based on a teacher's highest salary during his last three years on the job, the EEA has had the effect of encouraging teachers to stay on the job longer. That trend, coupled with municipal budget cuts, will mean some of the younger teachers

who have been subjected to rigorous standards and testing as part of EEA will be losing their jobs" (*Daily Hampshire Gazette*, June 11, 1991).

9. Other controls in the model included age, gender, subject specialty, cohort, race, and district characteristics.

10. This is in accordance with the finding of Murnane et al., that the effects of salary on attrition are limited to the first several years of a teaching career. However, this result is not common to all studies of teacher attrition. For example, Mont and Rees (1996), estimating separate hazard functions for a sample of New York state teachers with less than four years' experience and a second sample of teachers with more than four years' experience, find strong negative effects of salary on quit rates in both groups.

11. The argument of this section is presented in greater detail in Ballou (1996), which includes several sensitivity tests.

12. A similar explanation was offered when a study of entry by North Carolina teachers showed that certificants with higher NTE scores were less likely to take a teaching job (Murnane and Schwinden 1989). While the authors note that the data do not allow them to disentangle the influence of supply factors from demand factors in accounting for this phenomenon, they surmise that candidates with higher scores enjoyed better options in the labor market and therefore chose not to teach.

13. These data sets include the National Longitudinal Survey of 1972 (Vance and Schlechty 1982; Weaver 1979; Nelson 1985) and High School and Beyond (Hanushek and Pace 1995).

14. Since the sample is restricted to certified graduates, this seems to be a reasonable assumption. Persons who intended to teach all along in a private school need not, in general, have invested time and effort obtaining a certificate. Nonetheless, there are some reasons to suspect that our results may be sensitive to this treatment of private school teachers. We have investigated this issue using a more complicated version of the model that estimates both the probability that an individual sought a teaching job and the probability than an offer was received. In this framework, there is no need to impose the assumption that all certified private school teachers were disappointed public sector applicants. The results were robust to this alternative specification. A full discussion of this and other sensitivity tests is provided in Ballou (1996).

15. To provide results comparable with those from the SRCG, we have restricted the sample to public school instructors with three or fewer years of experience.

16. As noted above, we have presented elsewhere a two-equation version of the model controlling for selection into the applicant pool (Ballou 1996). Results from this model are equally negative about the importance of college background in hiring decisions.

17. Interactions of GPA with education major are positive (though the effect of GPA is not significantly different for education majors and other majors). Thus, education majors are at least as likely as others to benefit from higher grades. Interactions of GPA with college quality are not statistically significant.

18. Case studies of teacher selection reported in Wise et al. (1987) indicate that these criteria vary considerably from one school system to another. Principals need to be persuaded that a given teacher will "fit in" at their schools. There are no overarching criteria that appear to predict employability across various school systems. If this view is correct, it supports our contention that prospective teachers find it very hard to assess their own prospects in the market.

19. Teaching salary structures are rigid even by the standards of the civil service, the other major category of government employees. In the federal Civil Service, for example, entry GS levels can be adjusted to permit differentials for professions or fields in greater demand. Once hired, all employees undergo annual performance appraisals, which determine the rate at which they progress within a grade or move up grades. Merit pay is used to a limited extent in the GS grades, more extensively at managerial levels (Milkovich and Wigdor 1991).

20. Although the State of Connecticut claims that salary reforms and stricter licensing standards have led to improvements in the quality of its workforce, it does not report the kind of data that would allow this claim to be verified. Since 1988-89, the state has published biannual data on "newly hired" educators, a category that includes former teachers returning to work and teachers migrating in from other states, as well as those newly trained in Connecticut who were subject to stricter licensing requirements (Beaudin, various years). This provides a very imperfect basis for gauging the quality of new teachers, who in both years made up less than 30 percent of the newly hired. Worse, since salaries of new teachers rose sharply in 1985-86, the state provides no benchmark for the quality of its workforce prior to the onset of reforms.

Efforts to obtain a more informative breakdown of the data from the Connecticut Department of Education were not successful. To some extent, we can make good the deficit with data on Connecticut teachers from the Schools and Staffing Survey of 1987-88. Of 353 full-time public school teachers with at least three years' experience who responded to the SASS, 10 percent had graduated from selective colleges. An equal percentage had graduated from the institutions we have termed below-average. How does this compare to the state's survey of its newly hired instructors? In 1988-89, three years after the sharp up-turn in salaries, the proportion of newly hired teachers who graduated from selective institutions was 9.6 percent, those from below-average institutions 11.4 percent. Thus, so far as we can determine, there was no improvement over this period. This changed somewhat by 1990-91, when the proportion of newly hired teachers from selective colleges rose to 12.3 percent, while the share from "average" colleges dropped by a comparable amount. There were, however, two confounding factors. Since the number of newly hired teachers also fell by one-fourth between these two years, it is unclear whether to attribute this change to changes in supply or greater selectivity in hiring. In addition, the state's economy was severely affected by the recession of the early1990s, a circumstance that may have increased the number of well-qualified applicants for teaching jobs.

The latest published figures are from 1992-93. At this point the state changed its reporting practices: the latest figures refer not to all "newly hired" but to beginning teachers only. Of this group, 14 percent had graduated from selective colleges. While this would appear to constitute evidence of improvement, these figures are not directly comparable to those reported earlier. Since graduates of the best colleges have higher rates of attrition, they are better-represented among beginning teachers. Indeed, the state's own published data on teachers newly hired by urban school systems show as much. In the 1990 school year, 18.2 percent of the experienced teachers who were newly hired by these districts had attended selective colleges. Among novice teachers who went to work in the same districts, the share was 28.5 percent. (Unfortunately, the state provides this breakdown only for these districts in this year.) Indeed, if this difference were to characterize the state as a whole, and not just its urban school systems, one would expect to see a much higher share of graduates from selective colleges in the 1992-93 figures. The fact that only 14 percent of newly trained teachers had such a background suggests that quality in this pool actually declined between 1990 and 1992. One must be cautious, of course, in extrapolating patterns from the urban school systems to the rest of the state. But certainly one would also want to be very cautious in claiming that the state has seen much improvement in the quality of newly recruited teachers, at least by this measure.

Appendix 4A
Teacher Attrition and Demand for New Teachers

Model

To analyze the impact of attrition on new teacher demand, we construct a model of the composition of the workforce by cohorts.

Assumptions:

1. There are T teaching positions, identical with respect to pay scale and working conditions.

2. An individual's working life lasts M years. Every year a cohort of N workers comes onto the labor market, some of whom fill vacancies in order to bring the workforce back up to T. There are no subsequent opportunities to enter the occupation.

3. Each teacher makes an annual decision whether to continue teaching. Exits are permanent. Thus there are no interrupted spells of employment.

Notation

P_s = the probability that a teacher who has taught for s years decides to remain a teacher for one more year (hence, P_s is one minus the year s hazard rate)

π_t = the probability that an individual remains a teacher at least through t years (t >1)=$\Pi_{s=1, t-1}P_s$

P_0 = the probability of entering the profession (becoming a first-year teacher);

T = the total number of teaching positions to be filled

N = the size of a graduating cohort (normalized to one)

M = maximum length of a teaching career (=40 years)

We assume that empirical frequencies equal the corresponding probabilities (a large numbers assumption). It follows that the total size of the workforce in a steady state satisfies

$$T = P_0[\Sigma_{t=2,M} \pi_t + 1],$$

where the right-hand side merely sums the (normalized) number of teachers in each cohort over the number of cohorts active in the workforce. P_0, the number of new teachers, solves as

(1) $P_0 = T/[\Sigma\, \pi_t + 1]$.

To simulate the impact of a salary change on P_0, we make various assumptions about the effect of higher pay on the P_t, $t>0$, compute the resulting π_t, and use (1) to find the residual demand for new teachers. To project P_0 over a multiyear period, we iterate this procedure, updating the π_t year by year.

Calibration

The behavioral parameters take the following baseline values:

$P_1 = .7$
$P_2 = .85$
P_3 through $P_6 = .95$
P_7 through $P_{30} = .98$
P_{31} through $P_{40} = .9$

In the first simulation, corresponding to the uppermost curve in figure 4.2, retention probabilities during the first six years are increased by 3 percent (e.g., P_1 increases from .7 to .721). Since the simulation is intended to mimic the impact of a 12 percent salary increase on attrition, this is equivalent to assuming a retention elasticity of .25 during the first phase of a worklife, and 0 thereafter. The implied five-year survival rate increases from 51 percent to 59 percent, a change well within the ranges reported in Murnane et al. (1991).

In the second simulation, corresponding to the middle curve in figure 4.2, we retain the changes made in the first simulation. In addition, P_7 through P_{30} increase to .9849 (an elasticity of .04), while P_{31} through P_{40} increase to .927 (an elasticity of .25). The five-year survival rate is unchanged from the first simulation, since the values of P_t, $t<7$ have not changed.

In the third simulation, corresponding to the lowest curve in figure 4.2, we increase P_t, $t<7$ by 5 percent and P_t for $7 < t < 30$ by 1 percent. The five-year survival rate increases from .51 to .65.

Nonidentical Cohorts

In the foregoing model the workforce initially exhibits a steady-state composition, in which every cohort follows an identical career trajectory. This trajectory is perfectly mirrored in the composition of the workforce: thus there are more new teachers than second-year teachers, more second-year teachers than third, and so on. This was notably not the appearance of the U.S. workforce in the 1980s, which contained disproportionately many teachers in mid-career who were hired during years of rising enrollments. As a check on the relevance of our initial analysis, we have recalibrated the model allowing for mid-career cohorts that were 50 percent larger (at the time of entry) than other cohorts now in the early or late stages of their careers. The results show that the relative decline in the demand for new teachers is virtually the same under the modified model as under the original assumptions.

Reentry of Former Teachers

Assumption 3 abstracts from the fact that many teaching careers are interrupted. In a steady state, this is an innocuous abstraction, since we can regard the retention rates in the model as net of such flows. However, for the purposes of this analysis, we need to recognize the existence of a pool of former teachers who would not return to teaching in the absence of a pay raise, but who might reenter the profession in response to higher salaries. Since reentry further depresses the demand for newly trained teachers, the estimates we report are upper bounds on the number of new teachers who will be hired following a pay raise. Indeed, under the reasonable assumption that turnover will be lower among reentering teachers (who are already familiar with working conditions) than among newly trained teachers, demand for the latter will decline by more than one for each former teacher who returns.

Appendix 4B
A Model of Turnover and Workforce Quality

Description

Denote teachers of low quality as type 1, those of high quality as type 2. P_{it} denotes the probability that a teacher of type i chooses to remain in teaching another year, given he or she has taught for t - 1 years already, while π_{is} is the s-year survival rate, the product of the P_{it} from t = 1 to t = s - 1. (P_{i1} = 1 by definition.) To abstract from temporary withdrawals, teachers who have exited do not return. Finally, q_{it} denotes teacher quality or effectiveness, varying across types and over time. During the first years of teaching q_{it} is rising, after which it stabilizes at a value assumed constant over the rest of the worklife.

The object is to contrast two policies, one staffing a teaching position with instructors of low quality, the other hiring only high-quality teachers. Mean quality under a policy of hiring teachers of type i is

$$\Sigma_{t=1,40} \ q_{it} \ \pi_{it} \ / \Sigma_{t=1,40} \ \pi_{it}$$

given a worklife of forty years. After n years, teachers of each type reach their full effectiveness (q_i). Effectiveness when first hired is a fraction of this, i.e., $q_{i1} = bq_i$, b < 1. In every year through year n, they gain a constant fraction of the difference between initial and final effectiveness. (In reality, on-the-job learning is front-loaded; the assumption that it occurs in constant increments biases the conclusion in favor of teachers with lower attrition rates.) Effectiveness of type 1 teachers is a constant fraction of the effectiveness of type 2 teachers with the same experience: $q_{1t} = kq_{2t}$ for all t, k < 1. Last, the attrition rate for teachers of low quality is a fraction of that for teachers of high quality at the same point in their careers: $P_{1t} = rP_{2t}$ for all t.

Apart from the P_{it}, the key parameters of the model are k, r, n, and b. If we fix b, n, and r in accordance with the results of investigations of teacher attrition and the contribution of experience to teacher performance, we can solve for the value of k (the relative quality of the two types) necessary to justify a policy that gives preference to low-quality applicants.

Calibration

Values of P_{it} are set to produce survival rates consistent with findings in the literature on attrition (e.g., Murnane et al. 1991). For type 1, P_{12} through P_{17} = {.85, .85, .95, .95, .98, .98} yielding a seven-year survival rate of .63. P_{1t} remains .98 thereafter until t = 30, at which time it drops to .9. The mean spell length in teaching is 18.6 years. To obtain values for type 2, r is set to .9 for the first six years, thereafter to .95. This gives a seven-year survival rate of .33 and a mean spell length of 7.9 years. In the baseline case, b = .5. For sensitivity analysis it is reset to .2.

Appendix 4C
Wages, Career Choices and the Composition of the Applicant Pool with Respect to Ability

The Model

We employ a simple model of the prospective teacher's career choice. Although actual career choices involve several decisions (whether to enroll in a teacher education program, whether to apply for a job, whether to accept any offers), we will collapse these distinctions and speak of a single decision to undertake teacher training and pursue a teaching career. This choice is made while an individual is still in college. We abstract from decisions to enter teaching at later stages in one's worklife, though such choices could be included via straightforward modification of the model.

Certified individuals who obtain a teaching job following graduation have an expected lifetime income of V, which is a function of teaching salaries plus nonpecuniary benefits (e.g., long summer vacations); V includes, of course, the option value of switching to another career at a later point in one's worklife.

There are two alternatives to teaching. Noncertified graduates pursue an alternative career from the outset, earning A over the course of a lifetime. Those who acquire certificates but fail to obtain a teaching job enter a fallback career in which they earn A-C, where C represents the opportunity cost of teacher training.[1] Such costs arise because students must forgo other coursework and/ or internships in order to complete the pedagogy courses and student teaching practicum needed for a certificate. Alternatively, a student may preserve his or her outside options in full, but only at the cost of prolonging his education in order to complete additional requirements for certification.

Agents are assumed to maximize expected lifetime earnings, inclusive of nonpecuniary benefits. A college student therefore elects to pursue a teaching career when

(1) $\quad \pi V + (1-\pi)(A-C) > A$

where π denotes the probability that a teaching position is obtained ("offer rate"). To keep the analysis tractable, we make the following simplifying assumptions.

1. Individuals are distinguished by two characteristics, a taste for teaching called the nonpecuniary benefits of teaching, τ, and ability, α. $E(\tau|\alpha)$ need not

equal the unconditional expectation $E(\tau)$; however, we assume that second moments of the distribution of τ are independent of α (as would be the case if, for example, τ and α were bivariate normal). The earnings expected in an alternative career and the opportunity costs of certification (A and C, respectively) are increasing functions of ability but are independent of τ.

2. The offer rate, π, is invariant with respect to ability.

3. Teachers earn an annual wage of w and annual nonpecuniary benefits of τ. Both are also assumed constant over time for any individual.

4. The expected length of a teaching career, S, is the same for all persons of a given level of ability, as are expected earnings when one leaves teaching.

Assumption 1 captures the essential features of this career choice, in which individuals weigh the satisfaction provided by teaching against the higher financial rewards that may be available in other occupations. In Assumption 3 we have abstracted from salary growth. The assumption that τ is constant over time is restrictive in this context, but much less so in the refined model presented further on.

Assumption 4 is primarily an expositional convenience, since we relax it below. It is easiest first, however, to derive our results under this simplification. It may be worth noting that Assumption 4 is not so far-fetched as it first appears. To be sure, some persons are more drawn to teaching than others and are likely to remain teachers longer. However, individuals are not well-informed about the strength of others' interest in teaching, and are therefore unlikely to know whether their own interest is stronger than average or not. Thus, a prospective teacher wondering how long he or she will remain interested in teaching might well take the mean spell among persons of his or her own ability level as a guide.

The assumption that π is independent of ability follows, of course, from our findings that quality of college attended and academic degrees had no influence on applicants' chances on the teacher labor market. Thus districts are effectively hiring at random. In these circumstances, higher pay can produce an improvement in the quality of new recruits (by these indicators) only if it raises the average quality of the applicant pool.

Since our interest is in the composition of the applicant pool by ability, we select two levels of α, high and low, and conduct the analysis conditional on these values (represented henceforth by the superscripts H and L). Let S^L denote the mean career length of low ability individuals, and S^H the mean spell length among high ability persons. It follows from Assumption 3 that the ex ante value of a teaching career, V, is equal to

(2) $V^i = (w+\tau)S^i + b^i(M-S^i)$ i=H,L

where b^i represents annual earnings in the career to which the teacher devotes the other $M-S^i$ years of his working life. (Discounting is implicit.) Substituting V^i into (1) yields the probability that an individual elects a teaching career, P^i_0, as

(3) $P^i_0 = \text{Prob}(\tau > (((1-\pi)/\pi)C^i - S^i w - b(M-S^i) + A^i)/S^i)$.

The term to the right of the inequality represents a threshold value of τ, call it τ^i, which must be exceeded before someone of ability level i decides on a teaching career; that is,

$P^i_0 = \int_{\tau^i} g^i(\tau)\, d\tau$

where g^i is the probability density function of τ conditional on α^i. Given our previous assumptions, τ will be greater on average among high ability applicants than low. Persons with attractive career options who choose to teach do so because they expect higher job satisfaction; the lower one's ability, the more likely one is to be attracted by the salary.

We are now in a position to investigate the effect of a wage change on the composition of the applicant pool by ability. There are two channels by which higher pay affects P. First, V rises. Second, since job vacancies are declining at the same time the supply of applicants increases, π falls. This feeds back upon application decisions. Differentiating P with respect to w and π yields

(4a) $\partial P^i_0 / \partial w = g^i(\tau^i)$

and

(4b) $\partial P^i_0 / \partial \pi = (1/\pi^2)(C^i/S^i)\, g^i(\tau^i)$.

Since the applicant pool improves if the increase in application rates is proportionately greater among persons of high ability than low, we convert (4a) and (4b) into partial elasticities,

(5a) $\varepsilon^i_{p,w} = g^i(\tau^i))(w/P^i_0)$

(5b) $\varepsilon^i_{p,\pi} = (1/\pi)\,(C^i/S^i)\,g^i(\tau^i)/P^i_0$.

Combining these expressions, we obtain the total wage elasticity as

(5c) $\varepsilon^i_{t,w} = \varepsilon^i_{p,w} + \varepsilon^i_{p,\pi}\,\varepsilon^i_{\pi,w}$

where the final term represents the elasticity of the offer rate, π, with respect to the wage.[2]

We want to examine the conditions under which $\varepsilon^L_{t,w} > \varepsilon^H_{t,w}$, implying a deterioration in the quality of the applicant pool. The following ratios are useful:

(6a) $\qquad \dfrac{\varepsilon^L_{p,w}}{\varepsilon^H_{p,w}} = \dfrac{g^L/(P^L_0)}{g^H/(P^H_0)} \equiv k_1$

(6b) $\qquad \dfrac{\varepsilon^L_{p,\pi}}{\varepsilon^H_{p,\pi}} = \dfrac{C^L\,g^L/(P^L_0\,S^L)}{C^H\,g^H/(P^H_0\,S^H)} \equiv k_2$

(6c) $\qquad \dfrac{\varepsilon^H_{p,\pi}}{\varepsilon^H_{p,w}} = \dfrac{C^H}{S^H\,\pi w} \equiv k_3$.

Using (5c), we obtain after some algebraic manipulation

(7) $\varepsilon^L_{t,w} - \varepsilon^H_{t,w} = \varepsilon^H_{p,w}\,[k_1 - 1 + k_3(k_2-1)\varepsilon_{\pi,w}]$.

The sign of (7) can be obtained by evaluating the terms inside the square brackets. Moreover, if the bracketed expression is close to zero, even a large partial wage elasticity, $\varepsilon^H_{p,w}$ is consistent with our finding that higher pay has produced little change in the composition of the workforce. Teacher supply might be quite responsive to changes in the wage, yet the full effects of higher salaries, allowing for feedbacks through π, remain quite small.

Evaluation of elasticities

To evaluate (7), we will identify graduates of the nation's least selective four-year colleges as "low ability" and graduates of selective institutions as "high ability." Data on teacher attrition suggest that the mean teaching career among type L persons is approximately sixteen years, while the mean among type H is about nine years. Approximately 60 percent of all applicants have found full-time public school positions (thus $\pi = .6$). The probability that a low-ability individual pursues a teaching career is approximately .18, that of a high-ability person .06. From distributional assumptions, we can back out (to an unknown scalar) the values of g^L and g^H implied by these values of P^L_0 and P^H_0. For this purpose, we assume that τ is a $N(\mu, \sigma^2)$ variate. Thus $g^L = .26/\sigma$, while $g^H = .12/\sigma$, where σ is the variance of τ. Observe that while this unknown scalar affects the magnitude of $\varepsilon^i_{p,w}$, it drops out of the ratios k_1, k_2, and k_3.

This leaves, finally, the variables C^L and C^H, the opportunity costs of acquiring a teaching license and applying for teaching positions, and $\varepsilon_{\pi,w}$, the feedback of wages on offer rates. The costs of acquiring a license take a variety of forms. Some students prolong their schooling. Others forgo the chance to take courses that would enhance their marketability in alternative careers. For those selecting the former option, C^i includes the opportunity cost of the individual's time over the year required to complete pedagogy courses and student teaching, plus any out-of-pocket expenses of attending school. Those electing the latter course of action incur an opportunity cost equal to the value of the courses they might have taken. This is more difficult to measure, though it is reasonable to suppose it is positively related to the costs (in tuition and fees) of attending the institution offering these courses.[3] If we suppose that such individuals might have prolonged their schooling but preferred to complete teacher training within a conventional four-year span, it is reasonable to take the cost of an additional year of formal education as an upper bound on these costs.

New graduates seeking teaching positions are also likely to experience a period of enforced idleness as they wait for districts to make hiring decisions. There may be a protracted spell of underemployment if unsuccessful job seekers attempt to work their way into a school system by serving as a substitute teacher or accept temporary jobs in order to try again the following fall.

Whatever form these costs take, they tend to be higher for students at selective institutions. Studies of the determinants of earnings have found that graduates of the best colleges earn 20 percent more than those who attended the least selective schools (Solmon, 1975; James et al. 1989). The difference in tuition and fees between the most selective colleges and the least far exceeds 20 percent, of course, though some students at the former may arrange to complete pedagogy courses at less-expensive schools in fifth-year programs.

This analysis suggests that the opportunity cost of acquiring certification will not far exceed the annual earnings of new graduates in entry-level jobs plus the out-of-pocket costs of an additional year of formal education.[4] In addition, C^H is at least 1.2 times C^L. It is likely, however, that this considerably understates the true ratio. For many students at nonselective institutions, the opportunity costs of studying teacher education approach zero (given the decision to attend college in the first place). A study of the transcripts of college students at seventeen major universities in the south found that elementary school teachers took two-thirds more education courses than state regulations required, secondary school teachers nearly one-third more than necessary (Galambos 1985). The failure of education students to take more challenging courses in college has led many states to impose such requirements on would-be teachers (Toch 1991). Enactment of a binding constraint of this type implies, of course, that the marginal opportunity cost of enrolling in an education course is seen as negligible. For students with no realistic prospect of entering another profession, an education major appears to be an easy way of getting through college.

On the strength of the foregoing analysis, we assume (conservatively) that certification costs for high-ability persons are equal to what they might have earned as teachers during the year required to obtain a certificate, i.e., $C^H = w$. For low-ability individuals, we assume that C^L is only half this large. We also comment below on the consequences of relaxing these assumptions.

The final term in (5c) is $\varepsilon_{\pi,w}$. Since this term is negative, its interaction with ε_π lowers the total application rate elasticity. It is straightforward to demonstrate that $\varepsilon_{\pi,w}$ equals $\varepsilon_{v,w} - \varepsilon_{a,w}$, the difference between the elasticities of the vacancy rate and the application rate with respect to w. As we saw in connection with figure 4.2, a 12 percent increase in teacher pay might easily lower vacancy rates by 20-25 percent, at least through the first ten years following the pay change. This is an understatement of the change in π, of course, since it represents only $\varepsilon_{v,w}$ and ignores any response in application rates. Since $\varepsilon_{a,w}$ is surely not zero, an estimate of $\varepsilon_{\pi,w} = -2$ would seem to be conservative.

When these values are substituted into the formulas for k_1, k_2, and k_3, $\varepsilon^L_{t,w} - \varepsilon^H_{t,w}$ is shown to be nearly zero, indicating that essentially no change takes place in the mix of ability levels in the applicant pool. (Table 1 summarizes parameter values and calculations.) This result is, of course, sensitive to the specific assumptions employed here. Reducing the ratio of C^H to C^L to 1.3 would raise k_2, implying a very slight increase in the share of high ability applicants. On the other hand, if C^H were equivalent to two years' income at the teaching wage of w, rather than one, $\varepsilon^L_{t,w} - \varepsilon^H_{t,w}$ would rise to nearly .23 $\varepsilon^H_{p,w}$ even if $C^H = 1.3C^L$, implying an increase in the share of low-ability individuals in the pool.

Absent better information about the parameters of the model, these results are suggestive, not definitive. However, this is enough for our purpose, which is to show that the claims in the text do not require implausible assumptions about the behavior of prospective teachers. On the contrary, under quite reasonable assumptions, it is apparent that the feedback of higher pay on offer rates is strong enough to produce the results described in this chapter.

Appendix Table 4C.1. Difference in Total Wage Elasticities

Variable	Low ability	High ability
Teaching spell (S)	16	9
Probability of applying (P_0)	.18	.06
Implied value of g	.26	.12
Offer rate	.60	.60
Certification/application costs	.5w	w

Calculation of difference in elasticities:

$$\varepsilon^L_{t,w} - \varepsilon^H_{t,w} = \varepsilon^H_{p,w} [k_1 - 1 + k_3(k_2-1)e_{\pi,w}] = .006\varepsilon^H_{p,w,}$$

with $k_1 = .72$, $k_2 = .20$, $k_3 = .185$

A Refinement: Fully Optimizing Agents

We now relax Assumption 4 to allow for fully optimizing agents who forecast S as a function of their own taste for teaching, τ. To do so, we need to impose more structure on V while preserving enough of the original simplicity of the model to obtain interpretable results.

Assumption 4a. Certified individuals anticipate that the length of their teaching careers will depend on future comparisons of the full teaching income, $w+\tau$, with the income available in the best alternative occupation. The alternative offer for year t is expected to be drawn from a distribution with probability density function f^i_t. The subscript t indicates that this distribution need not be stationary. Indeed, it would be reasonable to expect a high degree of serial correlation in this series (e.g., b_t might be a martingale). College students deciding whether to pursue teacher education will not, of course, know the future values of the b_t; however, they are assumed to know (or at least have beliefs about) f^i_t. As a result, they anticipate teaching in year t with probability

$$(8) \qquad P^i_t = \text{Prob}(w + \tau > b_t) = \int^{w+\tau} f^i_t(b) \, db.$$

The mean of the distribution of b is increasing in ability. Other things equal, more capable individuals expect to have shorter careers. However, f(b) does not depend on τ. Given ability, taste for teaching conveys no information about future alternative wage offers.

Assumption 5. Prospective teachers who foresee an interruption in their teaching careers expect to be able to return to teaching at will (i.e., with an offer probability of 1).

Assumption 4a makes career length an endogenous function of w and τ. The assumption that τ remains constant over time is not as restrictive as appears, since changes in the attractiveness of teaching vis-a-vis other careers can be incorporated in the sequence of alternative offers, b_t. Note, too, that a high degree of serial correlation in the b_t implies that individuals will tend to sort into one of two trajectories: those who find out early that teaching is not for them and exit in the first few years of their worklives, and those who make a career of it. This closely accords with observed career paths. Assumption 5 makes job availability an issue only at the beginning of a worklife.

It follows from Assumptions 3, 4a, and 5 that the ex ante value of a teaching career, V, is equal to

$$V^i = \Sigma_t \, (w+\tau)P^i_t + E(b^i_t \mid b^i_t > w+\tau) \, (1-P^i_t)$$

while

$$(9) \quad P^i_0 = \text{Prob}(\pi V^i + (1-\pi)(A^i - C^i) - A^i > 0)$$

as before. Since V^i is monotonically increasing in τ while A^i and C^i are independent of τ,

$$(10) \quad \pi V^i + (1-\pi)(A^i - C^i) - A^i = 0$$

implicitly defines τ^i, which is, again, the value of τ on the margin of indifference between a teaching career and an alternative career. Thus we can write the probability that an individual embarks on a teaching career as

$$P^i_0 = \textstyle\int_{\tau^i} g(\tau) \, d\tau.$$

It follows that

$$\partial P^i_0 / \partial w = -g(\tau^i) \, \partial \tau^i / \partial w$$

and

$$\partial P_0^i/\partial\pi = -g(\tau^i)\, \partial\tau^i/\partial\pi$$

where $\partial\tau^i/\partial w$ and $\partial\tau^i/\partial\pi$ are obtained from (10) via the implicit function theorem. Since τ and w are perfect substitutes, $\partial\tau^i/\partial w = -1$. It is straightforward to show that

$$\partial\tau^i/\partial\pi = -(1/\pi^2)\,(C^i/S^i)$$

where S^i equals the expected length of a teaching career for marginal applicants of type i (i.e., those for whom $\tau = \tau^i$). Then

(11a) $\partial P_0^i/\partial w = g(\tau^i)$

and

(11b) $\partial P_0^i/\partial\pi = (1/\pi^2)\,(C^i/S^i)\,g(\tau^i)$

which differ from (4a) and (4b) only in that S^i is no longer the mean career length among teachers of type i, but rather the length of a teaching career among marginal applicants. Note that the simpler model presented above can be regarded as a special case arising when agents lack sufficient information on $f_t^i(b)$ to evaluate (8) and therefore set P_t^i equal to the mean among persons of their own ability level.

Evaluating elasticities in the refined model

Because marginal applicants have lower values of τ, they will have shorter expected spells than inframarginal applicants. Thus it is no longer appropriate to set $S^L = 16$ and $S^H = 9$. Without more information on the distribution of alternative offers, b_t, we cannot say how much the marginal values differ from the average. However, it is possible to establish some useful bounds. Since S^L must be at least as large as S^H, setting $S^L = S^H$ establishes a lower bound on k_2 of

$$\frac{C^L\, g^L/P_0^L}{C^H\, g^H/P_0^H} = .37.$$

Similarly, since S^H will not exceed the mean career length among type H teachers, a reasonable lower bound on k_3 is given by

$$C^H/9\pi w = .185.$$

Inserting these values into (7), we find that

$$\varepsilon^L_{t,w} - \varepsilon^H_{t,w} > -.05\varepsilon^H_{p,w}.$$

Since this is a lower bound, the implications of the refined model are very similar to those obtained above. There is not likely to be much improvement in the composition of the applicant pool; indeed, quality may deteriorate. For example, if S^H at the margin were 7 years, rather than 9, the lower bound on $\varepsilon^L_{t,w} - \varepsilon^H_{t,w}$ would rise to $.02\varepsilon^H_{p,w}.$

NOTES

1. C does not capture all the opportunity costs of certification, since teacher training can lower earnings after a teaching career has ended. Since these latter costs are not relevant for the analysis here, they are ignored in what follows.

2. It will be evident from (4a) that in differentiating τ^i with respect to w, we have ignored any effect of w on S^i; that is, the derivative does not include $\partial S^i/\partial w$. This may appear inconsistent with our claim that higher wages reduce job vacancies by inducing teachers to remain on the job longer. In fact, as we show below, when fully informed agents choose S as a function of w and τ, the derivative of P^i_0 with respect to w does not contain $\partial S^i/\partial w$. Since the current model can be regarded as an approximation to a fully optimal decision on the part of an agent with limited information, it is inappropriate to include such a term here either. (This point is made more explicitly below.)

3. This may include a consumption value ("a great course from an inspiring lecturer") as well as the impact on future earnings.

4. In fact, use of entry-level wages understates C, which is the difference in lifetime earnings associated with having to obtain a teacher's license and wait out the application process for a teaching job. This cannot be less than the earnings that one might earn during that year; however, it could well be more, if it delays one's entry onto a career path in which earnings in later years will considerably exceed entry-level salaries.

CHAPTER 5

Prospects for Reform

The argument of the preceding chapters can be summarized as follows. Teacher salaries rose substantially during the 1980s. Nationwide, the mean increase was 20 percent in real terms. In several states increases exceeded 30 percent. Yet a comparison of new-to-experienced instructors turns up little evidence that higher salaries brought about significant change in the qualifications of persons newly recruited to the profession over this period. The modest improvements that occurred were not limited to states where teacher salaries rose the most, either in real terms or relative to the earnings of other college graduates; by most measures, there was little if any association between salary growth and improvements in the quality of teacher recruits.

The explanation, we believe, resides in various structural features of the teacher labor market. As a result of rigid pay structures, raises have been awarded across the board to all teachers, regardless of effectiveness. Because tenured teachers retain their jobs virtually at will, the predictable consequence is a decline in job availability. This feeds back on the quantity and quality of applicants for the remaining vacancies (and, of course, diminishes the inflow of new teachers, delaying any improvement in the workforce that might occur). Applicant quality is affected because application is not costless: would-be teachers must invest in an occupation-specific credential—a teaching license—in advance of securing a job. The poorer are job prospects, the higher is the opportunity cost of this investment for those with attractive options outside teaching. These are, of course, the very persons one hoped to recruit by raising pay. Were the market to send a strong signal to these individuals that their services remain in demand, this consequence might be avoided. But no such signal appears to be sent on a systematic basis: applicants with the kinds of academic backgrounds that indicate command of subject matter and above-average cognitive ability do not appear to be any more successful than others in their job searches. Under such circumstances, raising salaries may fail to yield any measurable improvement in the workforce.

These features of the market would seem to explain, then, why we have found it so difficult to detect a positive outcome of the salary reforms of the 1980s. We do not want to overstate the case, however. At the close of chapter 3 we acknowledged that higher salaries might have had some positive effect on teacher recruitment that we were simply unable to detect. Similarly, despite the negative feedbacks that we identified in chapter 4, higher salaries may still produce some gains: a somewhat better applicant pool, more selective hiring, an overall improvement in the quality of newly recruited teachers, perhaps in ways that we have found difficult to measure. But whatever has been accomplished by recent increases in teacher pay (results that appear to be quite modest, at best), more could have been accomplished if the labor market for teachers did not exhibit the various structural imperfections described in the preceding chapter.

This conclusion has important policy implications. On the basis of the evidence in chapter 3 alone, one might conclude that salary increases have not been large enough, and that with further increases the United States will finally begin to recruit the kind of workforce we desire. American education is often compared unfavorably to public schooling in nations like Japan and Switzerland, where salaries are higher and where the academic qualifications of teachers are considerably higher than those of American instructors. The case for raising the salaries of American teachers continues to be pressed, presumably in the belief that only if we increase pay will our teachers meet comparable standards (Bishop 1993; Bok 1993).

This policy prescription is, in our view, a mistake. Given the structural imperfections in the market, further raises are likely only to yield more of the same results—exceedingly modest if not utterly negligible improvements—at high cost to taxpayers. In our judgment, further increases in teacher salaries should be conditional on the removal of structural impediments in the market, requiring significant changes in the way teachers are licensed, recruited, and compensated.

We are not the first, of course, to be interested in such changes. Recommendations of this kind have been advanced for a variety of reasons, some having little to do with teacher recruitment. Our purpose here is not to evaluate all of these claims. Rather, we are interested in these reforms insofar as they remove the various imperfections and rigidities in the labor market that have undermined past efforts to recruit better teachers. With this goal, we examine some of the more prominent proposals and the efforts to implement them in recent years. What is the outlook for complementary reforms?

Salary Differentiation

As just noted, when teacher salaries are increased across the board, job opportunities decline, discouraging prospective applicants and delaying improvements in the workforce. To avoid these side effects, raises might be targeted to new teachers, either by paying bonuses to beginning teachers or by frontloading salary increases onto the first years of a teaching career. For new recruits who borrowed to finance their college education, loan forgiveness would serve the same purpose.

Unfortunately, it is difficult to design a policy of this kind that will prove acceptable to a majority of teachers and still solve the problem. While small bonuses might be tolerated, raising the regular salaries of new teachers above those of more experienced instructors will not. In order to preserve a conventional, upward-sloping salary/experience profile, a large raise for first year teachers will have to be accompanied by a still substantial (though somewhat smaller) raise for second-year teachers, and so on. But this largely vitiates the attempt to keep vacancy rates from dropping, since it is in the first six or seven years of a teaching career that quit rates are highest. Moreover, even this sort of salary reform will be unpopular. The median level of experience in the profession is now fifteen years; a policy that restricted raises to (say) teachers with no more than ten years' service would leave the majority with nothing.

Alternatively, salaries could be differentiated on the basis of merit. Merit pay has had a rocky history in public education (as have other efforts to differentiate teacher salaries on the basis of specialized knowledge, market conditions, or superior performance). This is due in no small part to the opposition of teacher unions. Unions have lobbied legislatures against merit pay; when unable to block such measures outright, they have influenced legislation in ways that promote the interests of their membership (Uzell 1983; Brandt 1990). At the local level, unions have opposed school boards and superintendents who support merit pay (Hatry, Greiner, and Ashford, 1994). In the face of this opposition, merit pay plans that survived have often been converted into forms of job enlargement offering extra pay for extra work (Murnane and Cohen 1986; Cornett 1991). Elsewhere, the size of merit bonuses has been reduced to the point where administrators often wonder if plans are worth the time spent on them (Hatry, Greiner, and Ashford 1994).

The opposition to merit pay does not come from teacher unions alone. Educators as well as some economists have argued that because it is difficult to spell out the practices that make someone a good teacher, administrators are often unable to justify merit awards to their staffs. The tenuous connection between stated criteria and effective teaching makes it hard to explain why instructors were denied high ratings and bonuses. Those passed over become demoralized and embittered, impeding efforts to build effective instructional teams. For these reasons, merit pay plans that have not evolved into arrangements to pay teachers for assuming extra duties have often been abandoned within a few years of their adoption (Murnane and Cohen 1986). In one prominent study conducted by the Urban Institute, three-fourths of the districts that had been using merit pay in 1983 were no longer doing so when recontacted ten years later (Hatry, Greiner, and Ashford, 1994).

Given the negative publicity merit pay has received, it comes as something of a surprise to find that the record on merit pay is not unequivocally negative. The same Urban Institute study found many administrators and teachers who believed that merit pay had a positive influence on their schools. The fact that most plans have been abandoned within a few years is not necessarily a sign of ineffectiveness; plans are abandoned for a variety of reasons, not least of them costs. Merit pay has been particularly vulnerable during budgetary cutbacks because it is typically structured as an add-on to base pay. As noted, plans are also terminated following a change of superintendent or school board. Merit pay may not "work" because it is opposed by unions, but that is not the same as saying it is opposed because it does not work.[1]

Whatever the other problems with merit pay, special difficulties will beset a policy that relies on merit bonuses to raise the quality of new recruits. Prospective teachers will discount compensation that is contingent on future performance, given uncertainty whether and when such awards will be made. In addition, to attract significantly better recruits, the sums involved will need to be substantial. For the policy to succeed, many new teachers will have to earn more than teachers with much longer service, effectively creating an unacceptable two-tier workforce.

An alternative to merit pay would award bonuses on the basis of measured competencies, a policy termed "pay for knowledge and skills" (Odden and Conley 1991). Such plans differ from merit pay in that the desired competencies are specified in advance in terms of objective criteria (e.g., test scores on subject matter exams). We are unaware of any large-scale implementation of a compensation policy of this type. In some respects, such a policy might be an improvement over merit pay. Clearer criteria for awards would presumably help in the recruitment of new teachers, who may well know whether they meet the standard. However, unions would likely be opposed, given their resistance to the testing of teachers for other purposes. Since acceptance by rank and file would presumably hinge on the proportion of teachers deemed to have demonstrated the skill, pressure would build to set standards that most teachers could pass. Programs of teacher education could be expected to develop extra courses and practica for teachers who need to be brought up to speed and to exert additional pressure to ensure that persons who completed these courses were judged to have met the standard.

In summary, while the evidence suggests that compensation could be more flexible than at present, considerable opposition would need to be overcome before differentiation of salaries on the basis of ability could proceed to the point where it solves the problem with which we began: raising pay without triggering a substantial reduction in job opportunities. The history of efforts to introduce merit pay and other performance incentives into public schools does not leave grounds for much optimism.[2] A policy that drew some distinctions among teachers would be superior to one that relied solely on across-the-board raises to

attract better teachers, but the difference in practice is likely to be modest.

Lowering Entry Barriers

If the foregoing analysis is correct, it will be difficult to raise salaries
without reducing the number of job openings. At a minimum, this will
delay any improvements in the workforce. Yet the effects may be still
worse, if declining job prospects discourage more capable persons
from applying in the first place. Unfortunately, this is only too likely.
Public school teachers must be certified in the subjects they will teach.
As a rule, this credential is earned before prospective teachers know
whether they have jobs. If a position is not forthcoming, the effort to
obtain a certificate is wasted, a consideration that can deter them from
making the investment in the first place. Conversely, if professional
training could be postponed until prospective teachers were assured of
obtaining a job, a decline in job opportunities ought to have little effect
on the number of willing applicants. The fear of making a fruitless
investment in teacher training would no longer deter interested individuals.[3]

The usual route to certification involves college course work in an
approved program of teacher education. Much of this course work may
overlap with that in traditional academic disciplines, especially for
those seeking secondary school certification, but some of it consists of
methods courses (usually termed "professional education") plus a student teaching internship or practicum. In most states these additional
requirements involve a minimum of eighteen semester hours for high
school teachers (Burks 1987). Elementary school instructors and special education teachers are usually required to do more.

Though these requirements may not seem very burdensome (especially for secondary school teachers), they can constitute a considerable barrier to entry. The barrier is obviously greatest for persons who
have already completed an undergraduate degree and who return to
school at a high cost in foregone income. Barriers are also substantial
for students who begin thinking about teaching only towards the end of
their undergraduate years, with courses to make up. Other students

(e.g., those majoring in the sciences) are often required to take a carefully sequenced set of courses in order to complete their majors. As a result, they, too, may find it difficult to schedule the necessary professional education courses within a normal four-year period. If they are fully resolved on a teaching career, they can circumvent this problem by taking their subject area courses within a School of Education (obtaining, for example, a degree in "physics education"), but such a degree will be much less marketable should they find themselves at any point looking for a job outside teaching. In states that have increased required course work in teachers' subject areas, this option may no longer exist; there may be no alternative to a prolongation of one's undergraduate education. At the University of Massachusetts, for example, all prospective secondary school teachers are advised that the usual program of study leading to certification requires nine semesters.

The best evidence that certification requirements pose a genuine barrier to entry is the behavior of would-be teachers. Substantial numbers of noncertified graduates take teaching positions in private schools for salaries well below those in public schools. Part of the appeal of the private sector is the absence of entry barriers, offering new graduates a chance to see whether they like teaching before they go to the expense of acquiring certification. Still more to the point, as shown in chapter 4, certification rates are quite responsive to the availability of jobs. If certification were costless (or nearly so), it would be difficult to explain why job availability affects the number of interested applicants.

If certification requirements were relaxed, public schools would be able to recruit more widely. One might wonder how much good this will do, given the evidence presented in chapter 4 that schools do not recruit optimally at present. However, prospects for improvement are enhanced given that noncertified applicants are likely to be of higher ability. The reason is that certification acts as a reverse screen, imposing greater costs on individuals with more attractive alternatives to teaching. This is most clearly true of persons who must return to school or prolong their undergraduate educations in order to complete additional coursework, but it also characterizes persons who might have improved their marketability in another career (say, by taking computer science courses or learning a second language) had they not been required to complete professional education courses. The same considerations do not arise for students who would not otherwise enter a profession and whose alternative occupational choices require no specific academic training beyond the mere completion of a college degree (if that). In addition, attrition from teaching rises with academic ability. Thus, more capable students can anticipate having fewer years in which to amortize their investment in an occupation-specific credential. Finally, academically talented students are likely to find professional education courses intellectually unsatisfying compared to traditional liberal arts studies, or, at the very least, to anticipate an unsatisfactory experience, given the low regard in which such courses are held.[4]

To summarize, the barriers to entry posed by certification requirements are higher for more capable students with attractive career choices outside education. To attract such persons to teaching, legislatures might lower entry barriers in lieu of raising salaries. Or both measures might be enacted together, since a reduction in entry barriers complements a pay raise by blunting the deterrent effect of a decline in job openings. Still better results could be achieved by using examinations and interviews to identify selected individuals who ought to be exempted from traditional licensing requirements, thereby raising their representation in the applicant pool.

What, then, is the justification for requiring certification of public school teachers? Economists have advanced arguments based on information and agency problems to support licensing in labor markets that would otherwise suffer from a suboptimal supply of quality—variants, essentially, of Akerlof's (1970) analysis of the market for lemons. The relevance of these analyses for teacher labor markets is doubtful, as they rest on the assumption that the government possesses information private buyers lack. In this market, government entities (school districts) are the buyers of services, and could on principle have access to the same information about job applicants used by other government agencies to issue certificates.

Murnane et al. (1991) note that teacher certification has traditionally been defended as a protection against incompetent or corrupt school administrators. Indeed, certification was once the primary requirement for teachers; only later did states expect their teachers to hold a diploma from a four-year college. In those circumstances, licensing requirements may indeed have provided some assurance that teachers would meet a minimum standard of competency. It is far less certain they do so today. The indifference of many private school administrators to the certification of their faculty (see chapter 6) suggests that this credential conveys no information about teaching competence that is not readily available in other forms.[5] Indeed, even within public education there is growing recognition that the entry barriers erected by certification requirements are too high. In recent years, many states have instituted alternative routes to certification, most often for the purpose of easing the transition from other occupations into teaching. Although they differ in details, these alternatives typically allow new teachers to complete professional education courses while employed on a provisional basis in a public school system, usually under the guidance of an established, mentor teacher. As a result, few of the costs associated with certification need be incurred until a job is found.

Most alternative certification programs were started recently on a very small scale. Only ten states certified more than 300 instructors by alternative routes between 1988 and 1990 (NASDTEC 1991). Nonetheless, in several of these states, teachers with alternative certification provided more than 10 percent of all newly hired instructors (Feistritzer and Chester 1993). In these states, at least, a significant number of public school districts have been willing to hire teachers who lack prior course work in professional education. Indeed, in Connecticut alternative route certificants have been more successful in finding classroom positions than those certified by conventional programs, though the numbers have been so small (about fifty per year) that it may be unwise to draw broad conclusions about the demand for such instructors. Some of the worst fears raised by critics do not appear to have been borne out. Despite charges that these teachers would not be adequately prepared for the problems they will face in the classroom, the retention rate among alternatively certified teachers in New Jersey has exceeded that of new teachers with traditional licenses (New Jersey State Department of Education 1991). A study of the alternative certification program established by the Dallas Independent School District found that recruits generally out-performed new teachers from traditional programs. They received more favorable ratings from supervising teachers and teacher advisors and outscored traditional certificants on the exit exams required of teacher training graduates (Lutz and Hutton 1989).

Despite the promise shown by these programs, most have been designed in ways that prevent them from playing a much larger role in the preparation of new teachers. As noted, many programs are small. Readily identifiable bottlenecks—for example, a limited number of places in mandatory summer workshops—restrict the number of entrants. Such workshops themselves can constitute a barrier to entry if participants are not certain that a job awaits them. The Connecticut program is a case in point. Participants must complete an eight-week workshop meeting full-time during the summer, a requirement incompatible with most forms of full-time employment. Yet there is no guarantee of a job when the workshop is over; indeed, barely half have subsequently taught in the state's public schools (Feistritzer and Chester 1993).

Because alternative certification programs were designed to facilitate mid-career changes, many will not accept individuals who recently graduated from college (say, within the past five years). This precludes the participation of a younger, more mobile part of the workforce. Other programs, created expressly to meet shortages, allow districts to hire alternatively certified teachers only after a declaration that no regularly certified instructor could be found (Feistritzer and Chester 1993). In many programs, there is a major focus on recruiting minority teachers for urban schools. While these are worthwhile goals, they make it clear that alternative certification programs are not primarily regarded as a vehicle for recruiting bright persons into teaching without requiring them to pass through a year of preservice training. Finally, while lowering entry barriers is an important step, none of these programs deals with other impediments to the entry of older teachers, notably salary rigidity. Yet salary flexibility may be essential to attract individuals who have been successful in other careers.

A more radical reform would permit school districts to hire unlicensed teachers. Limited experimentation is underway with this policy. Some states permit charter schools to employ noncertified instructors.[6] Texas has recently begun a special program whereby districts may hire exceptional individuals whose backgrounds have been outside education. No course work in professional education is required. Contracts are individually negotiated; salary offers are not constrained by the schedule. Despite these promising features, it does not appear that this program will be a significant source of teaching talent. Individuals can be hired under this program only after a special petition has been approved by the Commissioner of Education; reviews are conducted on a case-by-case basis. According to the Texas Education Agency, approximately 100 petitions had been received by the start of the 1995 school year. While the agency would not reveal the precise number approved, we were told that it was far below the number of petitions.

Proposals to reduce or eliminate certification requirements are vigorously opposed by segments of the education community that benefit from current practices. These include the faculty of conventional teacher education programs as well as certified teachers and their unions. Restrictions on the size of alternative certification programs and the population of eligible participants may well represent an accommodation with these interests. Sometimes the accommodation is blatant: under the alternative program that awards California's University Intern Credential, the teachers' union in the district hiring the intern must approve the application (Feistrizter and Chester 1993). Similarly, conventional teacher education programs have been given significant roles in selecting candidates for alternative certification and designing program requirements. Faculty at these institutions have shown themselves far less receptive to reforms that by-pass them altogether (see, for example, the attack on Teach for America in Darling-Hammond 1994). There can be little doubt that these faculty will continue to function as advocates of "teacher professionalization" and to inculcate their views in the teachers and administrators with whose training they are entrusted. This raises the prospect that certification (or the equivalent course work) may remain a de facto prerequisite for many jobs, even if licensing requirements are reduced or eliminated.

The defense of traditional teacher preparation mounted by faculty in schools of education should not obscure the central issue. The question is not whether preservice training provided in programs of teacher education is valueless (though the attitudes of many administrators in the private sector suggest that it may be very close to that). Studies demonstrating that new teachers who have passed through traditional programs out-perform those who have not miss the point. Defenders of the traditional licensing system must do more than show this training is useful; they must show it is indispensable—that no reliable alternatives exist to identify individuals whom it would be better to hire without this previous training than lose to public education altogether.

Raising Standards

In the previous chapter we argued that an excess supply of teachers discourages individuals with strong academic backgrounds from pursuing this career, especially as such persons fare no better on the job market than other candidates. Yet there would seem to be an obvious solution to this problem, namely to raise academic standards for teachers along with salaries. Ideally, higher standards would improve the job prospects of better-qualified teachers while better salaries ensure a sufficient supply of applicants capable of meeting the new requirements. Various standards have been proposed: additional postgraduate education, more course work in subject areas, and a passing score on a teacher examination. Proponents regularly point to the success of nations like Japan, where teachers must meet exacting academic standards, and ask why American teachers cannot attain a comparable degree of professionalism.

Yet we are skeptical that it will prove possible to accomplish much by raising standards for American teachers, apart from screening out the illiterate and innumerate. Our skepticism is based in part on the proposals themselves. There is virtually no evidence, for example, that postgraduate education enhances teaching effectiveness (Hanushek 1986). While advocates of additional education sometimes have in mind specific programs of study thought to be especially effective (e.g., the Holmes Group 1986), such claims often lack evidentiary support. Nor is it clear how to assure high-quality programs in the hundreds of institutions that train teachers. On the contrary, requiring additional years of schooling before one can enter the classroom raises precisely the entry barrier most discouraging to candidates with a high opportunity value of time.

Many states have increased subject area course work for secondary school teachers. Some now require secondary school instructors to complete undergraduate majors in the subjects they will teach (e.g., history rather than social studies or history education). It is too early to tell what effect this has had on teaching quality. As of 1991, there was no significant difference between these states and others with respect to the proportion of new secondary teachers who had earned a degree in an academic major. Delays in implementation and the grandfathering of current trainees have held up progress. The long-term efficacy of this reform is also uncertain. Consider the requirement that all history teachers hold a degree in that subject. Well-intentioned though this regulation is, it cannot ensure that the prospective teachers bound by it will be as well-trained and enthusiastic as those who would have chosen to major in history before the regulation took effect. An influx of prospective teachers into courses they would not otherwise take may put pressure on academic standards and dilute the quality of training that history majors formerly received. This is the more likely given the low college board scores (SAT, ACT) among education majors. This is not to say that this reform will yield nothing positive. But there will also be costs, not least of which is the loss of information formerly provided by the self-selection of students into more rigorous and demanding majors.

This leaves teacher testing. The last fifteen years have seen a substantial increase in the use of teacher examinations. Virtually all states now test teachers at least once before they are granted regular licenses. Some tests are for admission to programs of teacher education; others are given upon the completion of such programs, as requirements for certification. Many of these examinations are tests of basic skills. No one claims that they select into teaching the best and the brightest, only that they screen out teachers lacking fundamental reading and mathematics skills. Virtually all states allow an unlimited number of retakes on any required teacher examination (NASDTEC 1996). The circumstances are often remarkably easy. Those taking the California Basic Education Skills Test (CBEST), for example, are given four hours to take the test; they can spend all four hours on a single section and complete the three sections of the exam in three separate sittings. Moreover, it is possible to fail one or even two sections and still pass by doing sufficiently well on the rest of the test. Of the half-million individuals who have taken this exam, 86 percent have passed. This rate is by no means exceptional: passing rates of 80-90 percent on teacher tests are commonplace (Childs and Rudner 1990). It is instructive to contrast this with the situation in Japan, where every year approximately 200,000 candidates take rigorous prefectural examinations for 40,000 jobs (Leetsma et al. 1987).

As easy as these tests seem to be, teacher examinations have been opposed by teachers, their unions, and other professional educators.

Many have expressed concern over high failure rates among minority candidates; indeed, the State of California has been taken to court on the grounds that its teacher examination is racially biased. This is by no means the only instance in which the disparate impact of an examination on minority candidates has resulted in a law suit. It is hard to envision teacher exams becoming any more rigorous in this climate. On the contrary, the disposition of some of these law suits points in the opposite direction, as shown by the settlement of *Allen v. Alabama State Board of Education*, in which the state agreed to lower required passing scores. Examinees who failed the tests were to be given a second opportunity to be certified on the basis of a formula that gave equal weight to test scores and college grade point averages. Finally, if these adjustments did not produce a black pass rate equal to 90 percent of the white rate, the state agreed that additional numbers of black candidates would be certified (on the basis of class rank) to assure a final certification rate within 10 percent of the pass rate among whites (Hood and Parker 1991).

Indeed, if the problem is the failure of school districts to give sufficient weight to cognitive ability when hiring new teachers, it is clear that teacher testing is simply the wrong remedy. Passing scores can never be raised to the point where schools will be compelled to hire the brightest teachers. Nor should they be. Opponents of testing argue with some justice that an individual's eligibility to teach should not rest solely on performance on a standardized exam. The cognitive skills measured by these tests are only one predictor of teaching effectiveness. Other attributes also matter in the classroom. More difficult examinations with higher minimum passing scores would screen out some teachers whose strengths lie elsewhere. In addition, tougher tests could produce local shortages. A standard high enough to force some districts to raise their threshold for new hires might deprive others of qualified applicants altogether, forcing them to employ permanent substitutes or resort to other stopgap measures that are worse than present policies.

Unfortunately, a more balanced approach, in which test scores are weighed with other indicators in the course of teacher selection, does not seem likely. The Educational Testing Service, which supplies nearly all of the tests, has validated the NTE (and its successor, the Praxis Series) for purposes of licensing only, not for hiring or retention. School districts using these scores for the latter purposes would be in violation of ETS' express policy.[7] Moreover, as federal court decisions require validation of any employment test, such districts would be exposing themselves to costly legal action.

Let us instead consider an alternative, to raise standards for students. Indeed, if schools were held accountable for student achievement, there would presumably be little need for teacher examinations or other licensing requirements. Schools would choose to employ instructors capable of raising student test scores (or other agreed-on indicators). Since it is ultimately student learning that counts, this policy would appear to accomplish all that could be achieved by stricter licensing requirements without needlessly tying districts' hands. In addition, higher standards for students would have a positive effect—so the argument goes—on the effort of students and teachers. Indeed, it is primarily for this reason, and not for their indirect impact on teacher recruitment, that higher standards are generally advocated.

Educational standards are much in the news as this book goes to press, and it may be premature to pass judgment on the final shape of reforms. Yet the obstacles to success seem even greater than in the case of higher standards for teachers. The testing of students raises the same concerns about disparate impacts on minorities as does the testing of teachers, with the difference that these concerns are intensified when the outcome is something as critical to further educational and economic opportunities as high school graduation. Perhaps the most doubtful aspect of this policy lies in the notion that our political system is capable of crafting a coherent set of objectives to guide local education authorities. This was, indeed, just the purpose of Outcomes-Based Education, a movement that has stalled due to public disapproval of objectives that seem irrelevant, if not actually inimical, to the aims of education as various segments of the public conceive them.

Outcomes-Based Education is not the only effort to establish standards for public education that has foundered in the cross-currents of American politics. When curriculum guidelines for American history were issued under the Goals 2000 legislation, a furious debate was set off over the political content of the guidelines, and the U.S. Senate ended up repudiating the standards by a vote of 99 to 1. The lesson was not lost on the National Council of Teachers of English, who issued curriculum guidelines for English that steered clear of specifics, prompting this response from a senior advisor to the Secretary of Education: "The report contains very vague and very general statements that don't tell parents or students what is important to learn and don't tell teachers what is important to teach" (*New York Times*, March 12, 1996). States have also undertaken their own standard-setting exercises, but these efforts often fall victim to many of the same political forces. The task is made all the more difficult by a strong tradition of local control over schools. According to the American Federation of Teachers, only thirteen states have developed standards clear enough to be used as part of a formal curriculum (*New York Times*, March 27, 1966). As a leading student of education reform has recently observed:

> The multiplicity of often conflicting goals, purposes, and intentions that have become commonplace in American Education will make it difficult, if not impossible, to establish high standards. The politics of education guarantees a veto to a broad assortment of interest groups, creates entitlements for others, and permits exceptions for still others. These are the very conditions that created the current educational system, in which schools expect little effort from students while offering them inflated grades and self-esteem. It is unlikely that standard-setting activities can be insulated from the interest group politics that promotes uniformity of practice and tolerance of mediocrity (Ravtich 1995).

Suppose, however, that it proved possible to overcome all of these obstacles and adopt a clear set of standards against which students would be measured. It still does not follow that teacher recruitment would improve. Schools might escape accountability if the blame for student failure could be placed elsewhere. High failure rates might be masked by manipulating the population of test-takers (e.g., exempting the learning disabled) or replacing standardized tests with more subjective methods of assessment under the control of teachers (e.g., evaluating student portfolios).

Even if accountability were clearly established, there would remain questions about the appropriate sanctions. In a market system, a school that failed its clients would not survive. No such discipline exists within public education. It has proven to be exceedingly difficult to withdraw resources from failing schools. Administrators and teachers in these schools argue (with some justification) that their prospects for success can only be poorer if they are given less to work with. Such measures are easily portrayed as harmful to students. Similar objections apply to policies that do not withdraw resources but rather make increased funding contingent on improved performance.

This leaves little choice but to hold administrators or teachers individually accountable. Of course, superintendents and principals are already largely responsible for improving student outcomes, though in some states the institution of tenure has made it difficult to remove ineffective principals. It is not clear what difference it will make to give students more standardized tests; the tests in use now show that students are not learning enough. Of course, if the adoption of higher standards were accompanied by a more vigorous effort to remove administrators whose schools were not performing at an acceptable level, there might be some impact on teacher recruitment. Department heads might be instructed to spend more time with job candidates. More applicants might be observed teaching practice classes. Administrators might go to greater lengths to obtain information about applicants who have graduated from distant liberal arts colleges. Yet it is also easy to see how such steps could be overlooked by administrators under pressure to produce quick results. In most schools, workforce turnover is simply too low to afford any basis for a rapid turn-around in student performance. Principals are likely to concentrate instead on policies that will elicit greater effort and better results from the staffs they have.

What of the second approach, holding teachers accountable for what students learn? It is difficult to link student achievement to the performance of individual teachers. Many factors influence the amount students learn, while the impact of teachers (for both good and bad) is not limited to the years and classes in which they see their students. The most that one might realistically expect from such a policy would be the removal of the worst teachers from their classrooms. Yet once again, there would seem to be ample cause at present to take such steps. While raising standards might increase pressure on administrators to act, unless the policies that currently make it so difficult to dismiss poor teachers were also changed, higher standards for students would be likely to have little impact on faculty quality.

Many if not most public school systems award tenure to teachers after a few years' continuous service. In addition, as public employees, teachers are protected against arbitrary dismissal (without "just cause"). Most teacher contracts stipulate that reductions in force be conducted on the basis of seniority. As a result, teachers with more than a few years' seniority enjoy an extraordinary degree of job protection. Complaints by administrators that it is next to impossible to dismiss tenured teachers for poor performance are commonplace.

Hard data on the costs of such policies are difficult to come by; as a result, discussion of these issues is based largely on anecdotal evidence. Estimates of the number of public school teachers who are incompetent range as high as 10 percent (e.g., McGrath 1993); the poor performance of many teachers on teacher competency examinations suggests that in some states this figure is too low.[8] Yet the number of public school teachers dismissed for incompetence is exceedingly small. The cost of such efforts is a major deterrent: for example, a 1993 survey by the New York State School Boards Association found that the average disciplinary proceeding against a tenured teacher or administrator cost taxpayers of that state $176,000 (*New York Times*, Sept. 24, 1995). As a result, it appears that most school districts take such steps only in extreme cases. A review of employment records for all public school teachers in Washington State between 1984 and 1987 turned up only 42 whose contracts were officially terminated (Theobald 1990). This is consistent with statistics from other states. Fewer than .6 percent of the teachers in 141 California districts surveyed in 1982-1984 were dismissed for incompetence, a figure that includes untenured and temporary teachers (Bridges 1992). It is possible, of course, that many more have been "counselled out" or induced to leave by the threat of an attempt to dismiss them. Even so, it seems clear that many instructors of doubtful ability remain.

> The ambiguity inherent in teacher evaluation and the job security of most teachers exert a powerful influence on administrators to tolerate the incompetent teacher and to avoid the use of dismissal. Although incompetence is sufficient cause for dismissing a tenured teacher, it constitutes extremely problematic grounds for challenging the tenured teacher's employment contract with the district. Incompetence is a concept with no precise meaning; moreover, there are no clear-cut standards or cut-off points which enable an administrator to say with certitude that a teacher is incompetent. This ambiguity poses a serious problem for administrators because the burden of proof falls on them to demonstrate

that a teacher is incompetent. Administrators can never be confident under these conditions that a Commission on Professional Competence or a court judge will uphold their judgment (Bridges 1992).

Unfortunately, recent history suggests that it will be very difficult to take away these job protections. For example, school boards that signed contracts with private management firms to run their schools (e.g., Baltimore and Hartford) have nonetheless yielded to union pressure and severely constrained managerial prerogatives in personnel decisions.[9] As a result, these firms have taken on failing school systems with little or no authority to replace the work forces they find teaching in them.

Legislative efforts to strengthen the position of management have also been affected by union opposition. The Massachusetts Education Reform Act of 1993 is a case in point. When the act was passed, supporters declared that teacher tenure had been abolished in the state's public schools. This claim was somewhat disingenuous. Although automatic renewal of contracts was replaced by the requirement that teachers be recertified every five years, this requirement can be met in a variety of ways that pose no threat whatever to a teacher's job. In-service programs and workshops, conferences outside the school, and courses in the state's universities are all approved methods. (Even auditing a course counts.) Important job protections remain. As a reading of the act shows, the term "tenure" has been replaced by the phrase "professional teacher status," which is granted, like tenure, to teachers with three years' service in a system. The due process requirements that have made it so difficult for administrators to remove ineffective teachers remain substantially in force. Dismissals are for just cause and require written notification with "documents relating to the grounds for dismissal." Dismissed teachers can request arbitration before a panel appointed by the Commissioner of Education. The outcome of arbitration is subject to judicial review. The act also stipulates that districts are not to lay off a professional teacher if an instructor lacking this status is teaching a subject in which the former is certified. Collective bargaining agreements that allow a more senior teacher to displace a junior one in the event of a layoff are not affected by the legislation.

The Massachusetts case is by no means exceptional, as a recent review of state actions makes clear (Lindsay 1996). The Virginia legislature failed to act on a proposal by the state schools superintendent to replace tenure with renewable contracts. Lawmakers in Minnesota declined to follow up the governor's challenge to "put a premium on excellence, not seniority." The California Assembly killed a proposal to replace tenure with renewable contracts. In states where legislation passed, changes were often minimal. Thus, in Pennsylvania, the probationary period before an award of tenure was lengthened from two to three years (and in South Dakota, from three to four years). After proposing legislation that would make it easier to dismiss teachers who were given poor evaluations, the governor of Ohio ended up vetoing a law that, in his judgment, made teacher tenure still stronger. In New York, the state school boards' association has been unable to find a Senate sponsor for its proposal to replace tenure with renewable contracts. According to the association's executive director, the reason is the opposition of the New York State United Teachers, which spent more than $3 million dollars on lobbying and campaign contributions in the 1994 elections, more than any other special-interest group in the state.

Conclusion

In chapter 4 we identified several features of the teacher labor market that have frustrated efforts to recruit better teachers. In this chapter we have asked whether these impediments could be removed, clearing the way for higher salaries to attract more capable persons into the profession.

The outlook for such reforms does not look very bright. There seems little chance that the compensation of new (or better) teachers will be allowed to rise significantly while the incomes of the rest remain unchanged. Barriers to teacher entry have fallen, but very slowly: programs of alternative certification provide only a small share of new teachers and are often circumscribed in ways that prevent them from competing head-on with traditional programs of teacher preparation. Though most states now test teachers, these tests are a far remove from the rigorous examinations taken by teachers in Japan and some European nations. Since even basic skills tests are being challenged in the courts, more selective screening does not seem likely. Other efforts to raise standards and increase accountability have yielded modest results to date.

This is not to say that none of these reforms will ever amount to much. They may well succeed in other terms. We believe that in an increasing number of districts, the single salary schedule will give way to salary structures that include a modest role for merit pay, eliciting greater effort from teachers. We expect, too, that the on-going debate over educational standards will raise what is expected of students and that student achievement will rise. Where we remain skeptical is in doubting that these measures will have a substantial effect on teacher recruitment. None of the reforms we have examined are likely to be implemented on the scale required to fundamentally alter the way the teacher labor market works.

There are several reasons why. One is the difficulty of designing policies of sufficient flexibility to meet the various goals served by public schools. The diverse needs of a heterogeneous clientele have also made public education a political battleground where radical reform is unlikely. Yet in our view, the major obstacle is the influence wielded by teacher unions, associations of administrators, and education schools in the formulation of education policy. These groups have strong vested interests in the present system of training and licensing teachers and in the terms of their employment. The consequences of their opposition are clearly apparent when reforms are blocked or repealed. Less obvious, but still important, is the ability of these groups to influence the policy-making process, shaping reforms in ways that serve their interests.

Twelve years ago, in *A Nation at Risk*, the National Commission on Excellence in Education advanced the following recommendations.

> Salaries for the teaching profession should be increased and should be professionally competitive, market-sensitive, and performance-based. Salary, promotion, tenure, and retention decisions should be tied to an effective evaluation system that includes peer review so that superior teachers can be rewarded, average ones encouraged, and poor ones either improved or terminated (National Commission on Excellence in Education 1983).

For all the effort that has gone into education reform since then, the nation is still waiting to see significant progress on most of these counts. Proposals that threaten the power of teacher unions or diminish the role of the nation's schools and departments of education in the preparation of teachers and administrators have been defeated outright or severely restricted in scope. In the twelve years that have elapsed since the publication of *A Nation at Risk*, numerous states have awarded teachers significant increases in salaries. Few, if any, have enacted the other changes needed to ensure that better teachers are recruited as a result.

NOTES

1. Other data show that many teachers are more open minded on the subject of merit pay than much union rhetoric would suggest. As is often the case, surveys have presented contradictory findings. Two Gallup polls conducted for the *Phi Delta Kappan* in 1984 and 1989 found a majority of respondents (64 percent and 61 percent, respectively) opposed to merit pay (Gallop 1984; Elam 1989). However, a 1983 poll of teachers by the National School Board Association turned up 63 percent in favor (Cramer 1983). A 1990 survey by the National Center for Education Information found that 70 percent favored pay on the basis of job performance in addition to seniority and education (Feistritzer 1990). Differences in survey design and the phrasing of questions are likely to have influenced responses and may explain some of these discrepancies. These polls also differed with respect to sample size, sampling technique, and response rates, further complicating the interpretation of results.

Additional information on teachers' attitudes toward incentive pay was obtained by the National Center for Education Statistics in the 1987-1988 Schools and Staffing Survey (SASS), which asked teachers their opinion of particular types of compensation and whether they received such remuneration. While it would be unwise to claim that any one survey provides a definitive answer to this question, both the sample size and the response rate were far higher for this survey than for any of those just cited. Opposition to performance incentives of any kind came from a minority of teachers. These data have been subjected to a multivariate analysis exploring the determinants of teachers' attitudes toward merit pay (Ballou and Podgursky 1993b). Teachers in schools using merit pay were more favorably disposed toward this kind of compensation than were teachers elsewhere. The effect was greatest among those who actually received a bonus, but attitudes were more positive even among nonrecipients. Teachers who were more likely to be working with students from disadvantaged backgrounds (e.g., minority teachers, employees of large urban school systems) were also more supportive, a pattern difficult to square with the notion that teachers resist performance-based pay because so many determinants of student learning are beyond their control.

These findings suggest that easy generalizations about teachers' views on incentive pay should be resisted. That teachers in districts using merit pay are generally more supportive than teachers elsewhere indicates that characterizations of merit pay as a frequent source of divisiveness and ill-feeling may be overstated. Indeed, a different item on the same survey asked teachers whether they agreed or disagreed with the statement: "There is great cooperation among the staff in this school." In schools lacking a merit pay plan, the response rates were 36 percent strongly agree, 43 percent mildly agree, 16 percent mildly disagree, and 5 percent strongly disagree. Response rates in schools with merit pay plans were 37 percent, 43 percent, 15 percent, and 5 percent. There was virtually no difference between recipients' and nonrecipients' answers in the latter districts.

2. One such incentive that has attracted much recent attention is the career ladder. As the name implies, a career ladder involves a progression of steps through which the teacher advances in the course of a career. It is fair to say, however, that proponents of career ladders have never satisfactorily resolved a fundamental tension in the concept: how to provide career advancement for teachers that does not remove them from the classroom. Some career ladders expressly require that instructors continue to spend the same amount of time teaching as they move to higher levels. This has the inevitable consequence of turning a career ladder into a form of extra pay for extra work. In most career ladders, moreover, eligibility for advancement is based on years of service and completion of workshops, courses, and/or advanced degrees. In this respect, ladders differ only modestly from traditional salary schedules, which also reward experience and education. Some form of performance evaluation is also a criterion for advancement, a feature that has proven problematic. When promotion is limited to a relatively small number of truly outstanding teachers, ladders provoke the same objects as merit pay. Indeed, dissatisfaction is likely to be keener, since the amounts of money at stake are substantially greater. On the other hand, in many instances meaningful performance reviews are not undertaken and promotion comes too easily (Hatry, Greiner, and Ashford 1994).

3. This is brought out by equation (4b) in appendix 4C, where the derivative of the application probability with respect to the offer rate is shown to be a multiple of C, the opportunity costs of certification. With C=0, this derivative is also zero: a low offer probability does not deter job seekers if no costs must be incurred acquiring a credential in advance of employment.

This is not to say that low offer rates might not discourage applicants for psychological reasons. However, a rational actor should not be deterred by a low probability of success, if the costs of applying are zero. Costs are not, of course, strictly zero; prospective teachers must send out applications, go to interviews, etc. These costs are trivial, however, compared to the investment in acquiring certification.

4. To say that undergraduate training in education is held in low esteem is perhaps an understatement. Boston University President John Silber writes, "The willingness to endure four years in a typical school of education often constitutes a negative intelligence test" (quoted in Finn 1991). Sowell (1993) concludes, "In short, some of the least-qualified students, taught by the least-qualified professors in the lowest-quality courses supply most of American public school teachers." An earlier, widely cited critique of teacher training by the president of the Council on Basic Education concluded that the subject matter taught at education schools reflected "intellectual impoverishment" and was filled with jargon that "masks a lack of thought, supports a specious scientism . . . and repels any educated mind that happens upon it" (Koerner 1963).

5. This conclusion is supported by estimates of a hedonic wage equation for private school instructors. There is no consistent evidence that these schools place a positive value on certification. Other measures of academic ability, by contrast, carry significantly larger hedonic prices (Ballou and Podgursky 1995c).

6. This freedom may be more apparent that real, if the authorities granting charters decide to require these schools to comply with the same regulations that apply to public schools. This seems all the more likely when the chartering authority is itself a local school board, the case in several states (e.g., California).

7. "As a matter of policy . . . assessment scores and other data from the Praxis Series may not be used . . . to determine employment, retention, or termination of fully licensed teachers. School districts without authority to license teachers may receive the Praxis Series assessment scores or

other Praxis assessment data of teacher applicants only to verify that the applicants have met the state licensing testing requirements" (Educational Testing Service 1992).

To validate the Praxis exam, ETS solicits the opinions of teachers, education school faculty, and other education professionals regarding test items. Respondents are asked what proportion of "minimally qualified" teachers would be able to answer a particular item correctly. No attempt is made to ascertain whether test scores predict differences in teaching effectiveness above the level of minimum competence. Nor has ETS made any effort to correlate student outcomes with teachers' scores on these examinations. According to one ETS official whom we questioned, opposition of teacher unions figured among the reasons for this decision.

8. During the 1980s, 10 percent of experienced teachers in Texas and Arkansas failed teacher competency tests that amounted to little more than tests of literacy. A similar failure rate occurs on mandated certificate renewal tests in Georgia. A basic skills test for new teachers introduced in Florida in the 1980s produced failure rates of 63 percent for blacks, 50 percent for Hispanics, and 12 percent for whites (Toch 1991, p. 164). Unfortunately, teachers are given so many opportunities to retake these examinations that few are actually dismissed. If 10 percent of the workforce cannot pass a basic skills test, the proportion who are incompetent for whatever reasons is probably considerably greater.

9. In an exception to this pattern, the Wilkinsburg, Pennsylvania school district has contracted-out management of a single elementary school to a private firm, Alternative Public Schools, which has been given the authority to replace current teachers. The local union, an NEA affiliate, has taken the board to court. As of this writing, a lower court order to rescind the contract has been stayed by the Pennsylvania Supreme Court, which has yet to rule on the legality of this contract.

CHAPTER 6

The Private Sector

There has lately been a remarkable growth of interest in the role market forces could play in education reform. At the heart of this argument is the claim that private schools provide a better education than public schools because they have been compelled to adopt policies that respond to consumers' demands and because they are not as heavily regulated. Public schools, it is alleged, could do likewise if they faced the same incentives and opportunities. Various mechanisms, ranging from charter schools to educational vouchers, have been proposed to empower consumers and provide them a sufficient range of options to make reform on the market model possible.

In this chapter we examine the implications of this argument for teacher recruitment and retention by examining the personnel policies of private schools. It is not obvious that a deregulated and competitive market, whatever its other advantages for consumers, will make it easier for schools to recruit good teachers. As noted in the preceding chapter, many of the regulations and contractual constraints that limit managerial prerogatives in the public sector are thought to benefit teachers. One might therefore expect private schools to labor under a disadvantage in recruiting faculty. In particular, few private schools have been organized by unions. If a unionized workplace is more attractive than one that has not been organized, private school recruitment will suffer.[1]

To conduct this investigation we turn again to the national surveys that have provided data for earlier chapters. We also report information and insights obtained from discussions with more than thirty school heads, diocesan superintendents, and officials of Catholic, protestant, and independent national private school associations. These persons are collectively acquainted with the policies and practices of hundreds of private schools, both religious and nonreligious, in all parts of the country. We have also interviewed managers and owners of several proprietary or for-profit businesses providing K-12 educational services. At various points below we draw on the comments of these educators to improve our understanding of the way this sector works.

Teacher Quality

Nationwide, public school teachers earn half again as much as teachers employed in private schools (see table 6.1). This difference is greatest in the northeast but is substantial in all regions. Part of the gap reflects higher levels of education and experience in the public sector. However, most of it remains after controlling for those factors, as shown by the difference in starting salaries (36 percent).[2]

Despite the differences in pay, by most of our indicators private school faculties are as good as those in the public sector, if not better. As shown in table 6.1, a higher proportion attended selective colleges. Fewer went to colleges rated below average.[3] The private sector employs more secondary teachers with an academic major and recruits as many teachers with degrees in mathematics or science (relative to its size). There is no significant difference in teachers' undergraduate grades.

It may be wondered whether this comparison favors private schools simply because so many of them are located in the northeast, home to many selective colleges and universities. However, a regional breakdown reveals a private sector advantage in all parts of the country. This advantage grows more pronounced when attention is restricted to secondary schools, where academic credentials presumably play a larger role in hiring decisions.

On a few dimensions the comparison favors public schools. More private school teachers lack a bachelor's degree, nearly 3 percent, as opposed to fewer than 1 percent in the public sector.[4] In addition, because turnover is higher in the private sector, mean experience is lower. More than 7 percent of private school teachers were in their first year of full-time teaching in 1987-88, compared to 4 percent in the public sector.

Table 6.1. Comparison of Public and Private School Teachers[a]

Salary and quality indicators	Public				Private			
	All regions	Northeast	Other regions	Secondary & combined	All regions	Northeast	Other regions	Secondary & combined
Mean salary	26,458	30,106	25,456	26,886	17,434	17,796	17,300	18,406
(std. dev.)	(7,278)	(7,928)	(6,752)	(7,510)	(6,035)	(6,546)	(5,830)	(6,329)
Starting pay	18,314	19,125	18,104	18,315	13,466	13,017	13,608	14,086
(std. dev.)	(2,267)	(2,173)	(2,243)	(2,261)	(3,073)	(3,039)	(3,070)	(3,081)
College								
Selective	6.5 / 6.8[b]	11.6	5.2	7.3	10.7 / 12.4[b]	18.7	8.0	13.8
Above-average	14.8 / 15.4	21.0	13.1	15.3	13.1 / 15.2	16.6	11.8	13.2
Average	49.0 / 51.2	54.0	47.6	47.8	44.5 / 51.4	42.8	45.1	42.9
Below-average	25.3 / 26.5	8.2	30.0	24.8	18.1 / 21.0	7.9	21.9	16.6
Unrated	3.7 / ---	4.4	3.5	3.7	12.7 / ---	11.5	10.6	11.2
No Bachelor's Degree	.7 / ---	.8	.6	1.1	2.9 / ---	3.5	2.6	2.3
Mathematics or science major (secondary only)	6.8	7.6	6.4	6.8	6.8	6.8	6.8	6.8
Academic major (secondary only)	38.9	43.1	37.6	38.9	49.2	60.7	44.9	49.2
First-year	4.3	3.4	4.6	4.1	7.6	9.8	6.8	7.4
Undergraduate GPA	3.3	3.3	3.3	3.3	3.2	3.2	3.2	3.2

SOURCES: Full-time teachers from 1987-88 Schools and Staffing Survey. Teachers in Catholic schools who have never married are omitted in order to exclude members of religious orders. Undergraduate GPA is taken from Surveys of Recent College Graduates for 1978, 1981, 1985, 1987, and 1991.
a. Percent of teachers except for GPA, which represents a numerical conversion of ordinal responses.
b. Percent of graduates of rated colleges only.

A final, albeit indirect, comparison of public and private school teachers is provided by the 1990-91 Schools and Staffing Survey, which asked principals and school heads to rate the effectiveness of their faculties. As shown in figure 6.1, principals gave similar ratings to new teachers in all four sectors: public, Catholic, other religious, and nonsectarian private schools. The modal response in each category was four. Intersectoral differences were slight and not statistically significant. For experienced teachers, the comparison clearly favors private schools (figure 6.2). The mean public school rating (4.24) was below the mean in each of the private school sectors. Significantly more private school heads rated their experienced staffs excellent.[5]

Figure 6.1   New Teacher Ratings by School Type

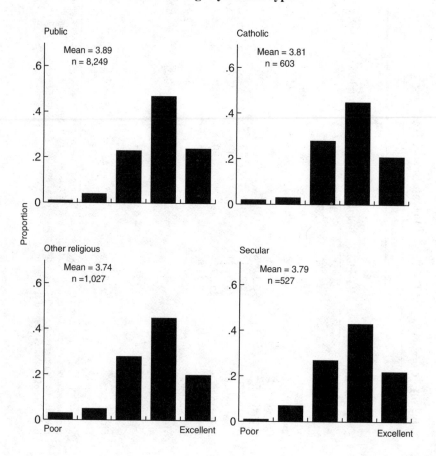

Figure 6.2 Experienced Ranking by School Type

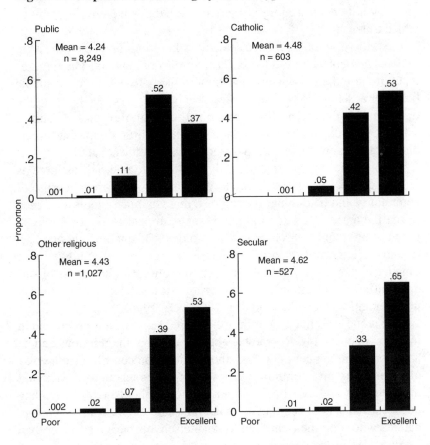

In summary, private schools appear to recruit remarkably effectively, given the substantial difference between their salaries and those in public school systems. What accounts for their comparative success?

Working Conditions and Benefits

Working conditions are part of the explanation. Generalization is hazardous, as there exist many types of private schools serving diverse clienteles. Nonetheless, the comments of administrators and the responses of teachers to national surveys indicate that private schools on the whole offer a more attractive and supportive environment in which to teach.

First, these schools practice selective admissions and enjoy the right to expel students who fail to conform to rules of conduct. The families that purchase their services are also more likely to insist on acceptable behavior at school. As a result, private school teachers face fewer of the disciplinary problems that confront their counterparts in public schools. Our discussions with educators leave little doubt that this is one of the reasons private school teachers accept lower salaries.

Private schools are typically only one-third to one-half as large as public schools at the same grade levels. Smaller size fosters a sense of community and belonging. By contrast, many public schools, designed to realize anticipated economies of scale, appear to be too large. A growing body of research shows that students at smaller schools, particularly elementary schools, have better records of achievement. Smaller high schools have been shown to promote higher levels of student satisfaction, attendance and graduation rates and to diminish involvement with alcohol and drugs (Walberg 1993).[6]

Size alone does not account for the shared sense of mission found in many private schools. Researchers have found that the religious beliefs and moral training central to a Catholic education contribute to a sense of community and common purpose that raises teacher efficacy and morale (Bryk and Lee 1993). Other religious schools as well as many nonsectarian schools can justly make the same claim. And, of course, parents who send their children to private schools have a stronger than average commitment to education.

Not surprisingly, these circumstances affect the way teachers perceive their jobs. In table 6.2, we report the responses of private and public school teachers to items on the Schools and Staffing Survey that concern relations with students, administrators, and colleagues. On every item, private school teachers were more likely to express strong, positive attitudes about their schools.[7] Particularly striking are teachers' perceptions of the support they receive from parents. Only 16 percent of public school instructors strongly agreed when asked whether they received a great deal of support from parents. In the private sector the corresponding figure was 40 percent. The importance of this question should not be underestimated: in the 1992 Metropolitan Life/Louis

Table 6.2. Teachers' Perceptions of Colleagues, Students, and School Administration

Survey items (1987-88 SASS)	Percent replying "strongly agree"	
	Public	Private
"School administration's behavior toward staff is supportive/encouraging."	40.5	60.2
"I receive a great deal of support from parents for the work I do."	16.0	40.0
"Most of my colleagues share my beliefs/ values about what the central mission of the school should be."	35.6	59.0
"There is a great deal of cooperative effort among staff members."	35.3	56.1
"In this school, staff members are recognized for a job well done."	25.5	39.2
	Percent replying "strongly disagree"	
"The level of student misbehavior interferes with my teaching."	33.0	52.5
"Routine duties and paperwork interfere with my job of teaching."	8.9	29.5
"I have to follow rules in this school that conflict with my best professional judgment."	40.6	58.2

SOURCE: Schools and Staffing Survey 1987-88. All differences are significant at 1 percent.

Harris poll of the profession, new teachers likely to leave teaching cited lack of support from parents more often than any other cause (U.S. Department of Education 1993). It also appears that teachers in private schools enjoy more autonomy in the classroom and exercise more influence over policies concerning discipline, curriculum, and student placement (table 6.3). They express a greater sense of their own efficacy. Seventy percent strongly disagreed with the statement, "I sometimes feel it is a waste of time to try to do my best as a teacher," compared to 54 percent in the public sector. These differences are also apparent in the responses teachers gave when asked whether they would still become a teacher if they had the choice to make again. Half of the private school teachers said they certainly would; only 37 percent of public school instructors were this positive.

Table 6.3. Percentage of Teachers Who Thought That They Had a Great Deal of Influence on Certain Policies, by Sector: 1987-88 and 1990-91

	Determining discipline policy	Content of inservice training	Grouping students in classes by ability	Establishing curriculum
1987-88				
Total	37.3	31.8	30.3	37.5
Public	34.8	31.1	28.1	35.0
Private	55.9	36.8	47.2	56.3
1990-91				
Total	39.1	33.3	29.0	37.5
Public	37.0	32.9	26.7	35.2
Private	54.4	36.2	45.1	54.1

SOURCE: U.S. Department of Education; National Center for Education Statistics; Schools and Staffing Survey; 1987-88 and 1990-91(Teacher Questionnaire).

NOTE: Teachers were defined as having thought they had a great deal of influence if they responded with a 5 or 6 on a 6-point scale of influence, with 6 representing a great deal of influence.

Compensation Policies

As noted in the last chapter, virtually all public school systems use salary schedules to set teacher compensation, with a teacher's position on the schedule a function of experience and advanced college credits (or degrees). Formal schedules of this kind are much less prevalent in the private sector. Only two-thirds of the non-Catholic religious schools set compensation according to a schedule. Among nonreligious schools the share is barely half.

Of course, private schools that do not use a schedule may still pursue policies similar to those in public education. Indeed, experience and level of education are major factors in determining the compensation of private school faculty, just as in public school systems. Often, however, these factors matter most when a school is making its initial salary offer to an experienced teacher. Thereafter, compensation may be determined in ways that bear little resemblance to public sector schedules. In some schools, all staff receive equal percentage raises as voted by the board of trustees. Faculty who obtain an advanced degree while employed at the school are much less likely to receive an automatic raise. A small number of schools negotiate contracts individually with staff.

Where private schools have adopted salary schedules, adherence to the schedule is not as rigid as it is in public school systems. In many Catholic parishes, for example, the schedule is an advisory guideline prepared by the diocesan board. Actual salaries are set locally by the pastor and his or her board and often deviate from these recommendations. Since the diocese typically runs the high schools while local parishes are responsible for grammar school education, there are frequently large disparities between the salaries paid teachers at the elementary and secondary levels, with the latter earning substantially more. By contrast, public school districts pay elementary and secondary school teachers according to the same schedule.

Policies also differ with respect to performance-based incentives like merit pay. As shown in table 6.4, nonsectarian schools are twice as likely as public schools to use merit pay, though the incidence among religious schools is lower.[8] Twenty-eight percent of the teachers in nonsectarian schools with merit pay plans are recipients, compared to 10 percent elsewhere. The financial stake is considerably greater. Although direct measures are not available, regression analysis of salary data from the 1990-91 SASS shows that a recipient of merit pay in the private sector earns, on average, nearly 12 percent more than he or she would in the absence of merit incentives. In the public sector, by contrast, the average bonus is only 2 percent. (Full results from these regressions are presented in appendix 6a.)

Table 6.4. Use of Incentive Pay

Incentive & coverage	Type of school				
	Public	Catholic	Other religious	Non-religious	All private
Merit pay					
Percent of schools with plan	12.8	6.0	9.3	24.3	10.9
Percent of teachers with plan	13.8	7.2	11.8	33.8	14.9
Percent of teachers receiving[a]	10.1	10.5	10.2	28.1	19.0
Average award, as percent of base pay[b]	1.9	---	---	---	10.7

SOURCE: Data are from the 1990-91 Schools and Staffing Survey.
a. Percentage of teachers in schools acknowledging use of such incentives who received an award.
b. Computed from coefficients in a regression of log of salary on schedule variables and binary indicators for incentive plans. Complete results appear in appendix table 6a. Too few observations were available to estimate separate coefficients by type of private school.

Private school heads find other ways to reward superior performance, assigning additional duties to good teachers (with corresponding adjustments in compensation). The boundary between teaching and administration is much more porous in private than public education: many headmasters, assistant headmasters, and deans continue to teach, while classroom teachers are also likely to be active as coaches, counselors, librarians, and resource teachers, and (in boarding schools) residence directors. Private school heads also retain considerable discretion with respect to the initial placement of a newly hired teacher on the schedule. Offers can be raised for teachers in hard-to-fill subjects (though few of the educators we spoke to indicated that they had needed to do this). Special discretion is exercised when recruiting individuals whose personal qualities make them attractive applicants. Individuals who are making career changes to become teachers are frequently credited with prior experience, albeit outside the field of education, in order to bring them in at a salary level comparable to that of other older teachers.

Surveys focusing on formal compensation policy will fail to detect many of these practices. To ascertain their importance, we conduct a regression analysis of the salaries of public and private school teachers to determine how much variation in pay remains after controlling for the standard schedule variables. Further controls are added for the overall level of salaries at the school, as explained in appendix 6a. Private schools that do not use schedules at all are omitted from the estimation sample. While a perfect fit is not to be expected—our regression equations imperfectly mimic schedules in actual use—proportionate *unexplained* variation in salaries is nearly double that in the private sector. This suggests that teacher attributes that we do not observe (but are known to school officials) play a larger role in determining compensation in the private sector. Of course, the additional variation in salary may not be related to differences in merit. However, the competitive pressures faced by private schools create a presumption that systematic differences in compensation have an economic explanation. Pay differentials that are unrelated to teaching quality lack a clear economic rationale.

The advantages of flexible salary structures are clear. Resources are allocated more efficiently. The adverse effects of across-the-board increases are mitigated. Since these benefits accrue as readily to public as private schools, there must be other reasons why salaries are more flexible in the private sector.

In the first place, private schools face market sanctions if they fail to attract and retain the kinds of teachers that sustain the school's reputation. No such discipline exists in the public sector. As a consequence, incentive plans in the public schools are more likely to appear as zero-sum games to staff, in which the bonuses awarded some teachers reduce funds that could have been used to raise salaries across the board. This is emphatically not the case in private schools, where improvements in the quality of the school's staff and instructional program enhance the school's reputation and increase the demand for its services. This feature of the private sector has no obvious counterpart in public education, where poor performance is as likely as not to be accompanied by demands for additional resources.

Many private schools have explicit expectations that teachers will become part of a team and commit themselves to serving the mission of the school. A private school teacher who persists in complaining about salary differentials risks being perceived as one who puts personal gain before the good of the school. The possibility of contract nonrenewal may inhibit the more extreme kinds of actions that public school employees have used to undermine incentive pay plans.[9] In addition, decisions about merit pay are often made in a quieter, less obtrusive manner in private schools. By contrast, the very formality and publicity accompanying merit awards in the public schools appear to alienate teachers, many of whom are anxious about the prospect of being judged before their students and peers.[10]

Recruitment Priorities and Constraints

Private schools face market pressures to provide satisfactory services to their clients. For many of these clients, a strong focus on academics appears to be a high priority. Students in private schools take more courses in the core academic areas of English, mathematics, science, social studies, and foreign languages. By graduation, the average difference amounts to two full-year courses (U.S. Department of Education 1993). This focus on academics is found in schools that offer a comprehensive curriculum as well as those that specialize in a college preparatory program. Indeed, private school students are more likely than their peers in public school systems to be enrolled in college preparatory classes even after controlling for student socioeconomic status, race, and educational aspirations (Coleman and Hoffer 1987).

The emphasis placed on academics influences how these schools recruit and how effectively they make use of the talents of their staffs. When asked what they look for in a prospective teacher, private school heads regularly cite knowledge of subject matter. (The other responses most frequently given are enthusiasm for working with children and, in religious schools, a commitment to the moral and religious beliefs of the school.) By contrast, public school officials do not appear to give special weight to a strong academic background when recruiting teachers. This difference in priorities is likely to be one of the reasons private schools obtain a comparatively high percentage of teachers from good colleges with academic majors.

Barriers to entry are also lower for private school instructors. In most states, private schools are free to hire teachers who lack state certification. Even in the states that nominally require certification of private school teachers, enforcement appears to be lax, and exceptions are commonplace. Schools often hire unlicensed teachers on the understanding that they will earn certificates within a suitable period (e.g., three to five years). This extra flexibility can be quite important to prospective teachers, who thereby postpone the costs of acquiring certification until they have determined how likely they are to make a career of teaching.

Data on the percentage of noncertified teachers employed by private schools are presented in table 6.5. Although most Catholic school instructors are certified, barely half of the teachers in other private schools are. It may be wondered if private schools recruit noncertified personnel only because they must, given their noncompetitive salaries. This is not the case. The share of noncertified instructors is largest in nonsectarian secondary schools, where salaries are highest. School heads in this segment of the market indicate in private conversation that certification is simply of no importance to them when hiring faculty.[11]

Table 6.5. Teachers Certified in Primary Teaching Field as a Percent of All Teachers

	Public school teachers	Private school teachers		
		Catholic	Other religious	Non-religious
All teachers	95.9	73.6	50.2	55.9
Elementary	96.7	77.1	51.9	49.2
Secondary	94.8	67.7	46.4	35.1
Combined	96.0	72.2	49.6	62.8

SOURCE: 1987-88 Schools and Staffing Surveys. Sample restricted to full-time teachers in states which do not require that private teachers be certified. Teachers in Catholic schools who have never been married are dropped from the sample to avoid including members of religious orders.

In the previous two chapters we argued that applicant quality would improve if licensing requirements were relaxed, since these barriers to entry are greatest for individuals with attractive options outside teaching. The data in table 6.6 confirm that private schools have increased their employment of graduates from selective colleges by recruiting noncertified teachers. This effect is particularly pronounced among teachers who attended the most competitive of these colleges and universities.

Turnover and Related Policies

As noted, teacher turnover is considerably higher in the private sector. Between the 1987-88 and 1988-89 school years, nearly 13 percent of private school instructors left teaching, twice the rate at which public school faculty quit. Another 4.7 percent departed for positions in public systems (Choy et al. 1992). There is little doubt the loss of so many experienced personnel adversely affects instructional quality in the private sector. Since private schools could presumably reduce turnover to the levels found in the public sector by raising teacher pay, it is curious that they do not. Is turnover excessive, indicating some kind of market failure? Or are rates of turnover that would be viewed with alarm in public school systems simply a sign of a cost-effective personnel policy?

High turnover does not appear to prevent private schools from meeting their staffing requirements. According to the 1990-91 SASS, 98.7 percent of all private school positions were filled by a qualified individual, a figure only slightly below the public school rate of 99.4 percent. Private school heads to whom we spoke indicated that they were experiencing no difficulty filling vacancies, even in such fields as mathematics and science. (The only reservation concerned the recruitment of minority teachers.) Freedom to employ noncertified teachers is obviously one reason. Private schools administrators also enjoy greater latitude in staffing positions when a qualified teacher cannot be hired on a regular basis. They are twice as likely as public school districts to hire a part-time teacher or increase teaching loads for current staff (Choy et al. 1993). This ratio widens to three or four when the comparison is restricted to public schools in large cities, where collective bargaining agreements curtailing managerial prerogatives are common.

Table 6.6. Percent of Teachers Who Graduated from Selective Colleges and Universities

College selectivity	Public schools	Private religious			Private Non-religious		
		Cerfitied	Not certified	Total	Certified	Not certified	Total
Most competitive	1.0	.9	2.4	1.4	3.4	14.6	7.9
Other selective	5.4	4.1	5.7	4.6	9.8	15.0	11.9
Total selective	6.4	5.0	8.1	6.0	13.2	29.6	19.8

SOURCE: Full-time teachers from Schools and Staffing Survey, 1987-88. Sample excludes teachers in Catholic schools who have never married.

Discussions of turnover among public school educators often convey the impression that turnover per se is never good and that the appropriate goal of policy is to drive turnover rates as low as possible. This is false; the optimal rate of turnover among teachers is not zero. This is not merely because older teachers can burn out and lose effectiveness. The optimal rate of turnover also depends on the quality of new recruits available to replace departing teachers. More capable individuals are less likely to spend their entire careers in teaching, creating a tradeoff between longevity and ability. We have already seen evidence that private and public schools view this tradeoff differently. Private schools are more likely to hire teachers with strong academic backgrounds interested in teaching for a few years.

High turnover can also be the deliberate result of policies adopted to deal with ex ante uncertainty about prospective teachers' ability. Such uncertainty requires that many candidates be given a low-cost opportunity to see whether they have a career fit in teaching, and if not, to move on. To mitigate the impact on students, new teachers require assistance and mentoring. In addition, persons who fail to recognize that they do not have a good career fit in teaching need to be counselled out or dismissed. The evidence indicates the private schools do a better job of managing staff turnover on both these counts.

The mentoring of new teachers is now widespread: by 1991, two-thirds of public schools had implemented a mentor program for beginning teachers. More than half (53.6 percent) of new public school teachers participated in a formal induction program with a mentor or master teacher (Choy et al. 1993). This was twice the private school incidence (27.3 percent).

This difference notwithstanding, instructors in public schools take a dimmer view of the help provided beginning teachers than do the faculties of private schools. Evidence comes from the 1990-91 SASS, which contained a series of questions concerning the assistance provided new teachers in four areas: student discipline, instructional methods, curriculum, and adjusting to the school environment. We have regressed teachers' responses to these questions on a dummy variable for school sector as well as controls for school level and teacher demographics. The sector coefficients are reported in the left-hand panel of table 6.7. In all four areas, teachers at private schools report significantly more assistance for new hires. Further evidence on this point may be found in the responses of inexperienced teachers ($\leq$3 years) in the 1987-88 SASS who were asked to assess the helpfulness of superiors and other teachers. Estimates controlling for type of school and selected teacher characteristics are reported in the right-hand panel of table 6.7: the results consistently favor private schools. In other regressions (not reported) we find that inexperienced private school teachers also report much more cooperative relationships with other staff than do new instructors in public schools. These responses suggest that new teachers receive more help and on-the-job training in the private sector.

Some private schools have instituted formal internship programs. Interns are generally hired directly out of college; they are paid substantially less than regular teachers and are assigned to work with one or more of the school's experienced instructors. At the end of the year, interns may be offered a regular job, should a vacancy arise. More often they are helped to find positions in other schools, including public systems.[12]

New teachers who show little promise should be dismissed. In principle, there should be little difference between the public and private sectors in this respect. New public school teachers are hired on a probationary status. They have no property right in their jobs and may be dismissed at the discretion of the school board.[13] Since it is extremely difficult to dismiss teachers once they become tenured, one might expect that public school administrators would make vigorous use of this probationary period to screen out ineffective teachers. Yet a 1984 survey of 141 mid-sized California districts found that only 1 percent of teachers on probationary status were given notice for poor performance over a period of nearly two academic years. To be sure, this understates the true extent of screening, if others were "counselled out" or induced to resign. Unfortunately, such practices make it easier for ineffective teachers to find jobs in other school systems.

In most of the private sector, by contrast, teachers are on "probationary" status throughout their careers. With the exception of some Catholic high schools where faculty have been organized, teacher contracts are written for one year and can be renewed or not as the school chooses. There is no tenure. While nonrenewals for incompetence are not frequent, they do occur. Virtually all of the school heads who spoke to us indicated that they had dismissed an ineffective teacher on at least one occasion.

Table 6.7. Assistance for New Teachers in Public and Private Schools

	"Indicate whether you strongly agree, somewhat agree, somewhat disagree, or strongly disagree that this school is effective in assisting new teachers in each of the following matters." 1=Strongly agree ... 4=Strongly disagree (standard errors in parentheses) Sample: Full-time teachers, 1990-91 SASS				"To what extent has each of the following people at this school helped you improve your teaching or solve an instructional or class management problem?" 1=No help ... 6=Extremely helpful (standard errors in parentheses) Sample: Full-time teachers with tenure ≤ 3 years, 1987-88 SASS			
Variable	(1) Student discipline	(2) Instructional methods	(3) Curriculum	(4) Adjusting to the school environment	(5) Principal or school head	(6) Department chair	(7) Other school administrators	(8) Other teachers
Dep.var. mean std.	2.12 (.93)	2.13 (.88)	2.04 (.76)	1.99 (.74)	4.20 (1.72)	5.31 (2.10)	4.43 (2.15)	4.64 (1.47)
Public	—	—	—	—	—	—	—	—
Catholic	-.278*** (.021)	-.181*** (.020)	-.252*** (.017)	-.268*** (.019)	.358*** (.071)	.681*** (.084)	1.428*** (.086)	.169*** (.060)
Other religious	-.303*** (.018)	-.138*** (.017)	-.227*** (.026)	-.279*** (.017)	.398*** (.058)	.626*** (.069)	1.009*** (.072)	.184*** (.049)
Secular	-.173*** (.028)	-.087*** (.026)	-.107*** (.009)	-.159*** (.025)	.033 (.070)	.258*** (.083)	.568*** (.088)	.141*** (.059)
Sample size	53,347	53,347	53,347	53,347	12,879	12,879	12,879	12,879

NOTE: OLS estimates. Other regressors not shown: male teacher, black teacher, secondary school dummy, years tenure at the school (columns 1-4 only).
***Significant at 1 percent.

Of equal, if not greater, importance for the quality of the workforce is the way schools handle reductions in the size of staff. In the public sector, layoffs are based on seniority. This is not the case among private schools. With the exception of some Catholic dioceses where contracts are collectively bargained, layoffs are never based solely on seniority (though length of service may be a consideration).[14] Rather, schools seek to retain their most effective teachers.

Over time, such policies can have a substantial effect on the quality of the workforce. For example, in a single year (1990), the contracts of 1.3 percent of private school teachers were not renewed because of budget limitations, declining enrollments, or elimination of courses (Choy et al. 1992). (Schools that closed and laid off all staff are not included in this figure.) If this year is typical, then over a decade some 10 percent of the workforce, many of whom have been deemed less effective than their peers, are put through a competitive screening process in which they must prove themselves to alternative employers or leave teaching.[15]

Market Forces and Public Education

To summarize, private schools employ a workforce that compares favorably with that in the public sector, despite paying salaries that are quite low by public school standards. While it's true that private schools serve a more select clientele, several other factors also play a role in this success. Salary structures are more flexible. Teachers may be hired who lack state certification. Private school heads find it easier to dismiss teachers who perform poorly or whose services are no longer required. Indeed, to a considerable extent, the reforms examined in the last chapter already characterize private schools.

Although private schools are subject to regulation, for the most part they are disciplined by the market rather than the state. To provide the services their customers desire, private schools emphasize academics and place a priority on recruiting teachers from good colleges with a strong background in their subject areas. New teachers receive more assistance than in the public sector; ineffective instructors are more readily dismissed or laid off. More schools use merit pay and other performance incentives.

Teacher unions, so influential in public education, are virtually absent from the private sector. Private schools are much more difficult to organize: they are small and diverse, with strong traditions of independence. Most are affiliated with churches and seek teachers who share a communitarian ethic difficult to square with self-aggrandizement. These are not, however, the only obstacles to unionization. Freedom to hire unlicensed teachers gives private schools access to a huge potential supply of instructors. Salary growth is constrained by the fact that schools face a competitive market for their services.

In short, the vested interests that have constituted such formidable obstacles to reform in public education play a vastly diminished role in private schooling. By contrast, consumers exercise far more power. In our judgment, it is primarily this difference—rather than any measured difference in the achievement of public and private school pupils—that accounts for the burgeoning interest in such market-based reforms as charter schools, educational vouchers, and privatization of instructional services. The resistance to change on the part of those who benefit from the way public education is conducted in this country has led many to conclude that the best hope for long-term improvement lies in the restoration of consumer sovereignty.

In any comparison of public to private schools, questions arise about the extent to which private sector performance is due to special circumstances not easily replicated in public education. This issue is central to the current debate over market-based reforms. Much of the clientele for private schooling consists of higher income families who provide stronger support for education at home. This is particularly true of students in nonsectarian schools. Schools with a religious affiliation benefit from a sense of community and shared values reinforced by the instruction in religion and morality. In addition, private schools practice selective admissions and expel students who fail to comply with school regulations.

Public schools, by contrast, must serve the entire population. They are expected to deliver services to all while simultaneously closing the gap between disadvantaged children and the rest of American society. Given the surpassing difficulty of this task, many educators regard the claims advanced for market-based reforms as fraudulent. Charter schools and private schools accepting vouchers, it is argued, serve few of the students who pose the greatest challenge for the public schools. Indeed, school choice plans are thought to make the job of the public schools still harder, as charter schools and private schools attract the best students, leaving behind those children whose parents lack the initiative or ability to find schools for them. The more closely the market model is followed, the more ruinous the outcome for these children, if public schools that lose students also lose resources. Given that the marginal cost of educating another student is generally substantially below average cost, funding cuts based on per-pupil expenditures will lead to a reduction in program variety and an increase in class sizes. Other negative consequences are foreseen. The departure of the best students will deprive the remainder of positive peer effects. Communities will lose some of their most effective voices for school improvement as parents most concerned about education opt for private or charter schools.[16]

These are legitimate concerns. Fortunately, a number of experiments are now underway that may provide evidence on these issues. These include a variety of school choice plans: interdistrict choice, magnet schools, charter schools, and both public and privately funded vouchers. Other market-oriented reforms include privatization of instructional and administrative services.

School districts have for some time subcontracted to private vendors noninstructional activities such as school bus maintenance and operation, food services, or facilities maintenance. A number of school districts now contract out selected instructional activities (National School Boards Association 1995). Indeed, the subcontracting industry has grown sufficiently large, and the range of activities so wide, that new contracts are regularly reported in *Education Week*, a newsletter devoted to tracking industry developments has started up (*Education Industry Report*), and the Lehman Brothers investment bank now organizes an Annual Education Industry Conference for investors.

The largest and most visible example of private sector subcontracting involves Sylvan Learning Systems. The core business of Sylvan Learning Systems is individualized mathematics and reading tutoring services sold to families at over 600 Learning Centers throughout the United States. Since 1993, however, Sylvan has signed contracts to provide compensatory education (Title I) services in Baltimore, Chicago, Washington, D.C., Prince Georges County and Dorchester/Talbot County (Maryland), Broward County (Florida), and Pasadena, Texas. In all of these cases, the teachers are Sylvan employees, and as such are not covered by the union salary schedules or the district collective bargaining agreement. None are tenured. Compensation includes performance incentives.

Huntington Learning Centers, best known for tutoring and test preparation services, has contracted for some time with public schools to provide SAT preparation courses. Like Sylvan, it has begun contracting with several school districts to provide Title I services. Berlitz Jr., a division of Berlitz International, has contracted with public schools in ten states to provide foreign language and ESL training. Ombudsman Educational Services Ltd. operated alternative off-site programs for at-risk students in grades 6-12 in approximately 100 school districts in seven states during the 1994-95 school year (McLaughlin 1995; Beales 1994). In response to poor student performance, the school board in Wilkinsburg, Pennsylvania recently contracted with Alternative Public Schools of Nashville, Tennessee to operate an elementary school enrolling primarily minority students. This case is particularly controversial since the company dismissed all of the incumbent teachers, hired its own teachers and aides, and terminated the union contract. This has put the company and district in a protracted and costly legal battle with the Pennsylvania Education Associated and its parent, the NEA. The final disposition of this case remains uncertain as this book goes to press.

All of these contracts have brought elements of the marketplace into public education. Contracts specify performance standards and hold firms accountable for results. For example, under its contract with the Baltimore school district, Sylvan provides 12 hours of free instruction for each student whose test scores fail to improve by a predetermined amount. Since public school officials decide who receives these services and on what terms, contracting-out raises few of the equity issues associated with parental choice plans. There is no change in the school's clientele, no creaming of the best students: indeed, the majority of these subcontracted services are provided to at-risk students.

That entrepreneurs stand ready to provide services to many kinds of students suggests market-based reforms need not increase educational inequality. Of course, the programs just surveyed are of limited scope and narrow focus. One might concede a role for privatization in these contexts and still oppose reforms that offer parents more choice of schools. Whether school choice will in fact exacerbate inequality rests, however, on several unproven assumptions. The first is that schools will selectively screen applicants, leaving many students with no effective choice. Failing this, it is argued that large numbers of parents will not choose responsibly anyway. Finally, public schools are assumed to be incapable of improving when faced with market competition.

There are not enough data yet on the way choice plans operate to know whether these conditions will hold. Some of the early evidence suggests otherwise. So far, states authorizing charter schools have prohibited selective admissions policies. While it might be better still to permit schools to specialize in serving particular niches of the market, if open access is deemed an overriding goal, there is no reason choice plans cannot be framed in those terms.

Early studies report that charter schools serve the same diverse population as traditional public schools. Of 106 charter schools responding to a survey by the Education Commission of the States and the Center for School Change (1995), 67 indicated they served a cross-section of students. Fifty-one served at-risk students and 37 the learning disabled. (These responses overlap.) On average, 59 percent of charter school students were white, 23 percent Hispanic, and 11 percent black. This is not to say, of course, that the students who enroll in choice schools are a random subset of the public school population. It is often argued that any choice plan is necessarily selective, if only because parents with the best information and the greatest concern for their children's education will be more likely to take advantage of it. There is obviously some merit to this argument; however, this point is easily overstated. Another early study of charter schools reports that "disproportionately many" of the children enrolled had fared poorly in their former schools (Finn et al. 1996) Rather than attracting those who would have been successful in any environment, these choice plans attract students who were previously struggling. A similar point was made in a recent study of parochial education: urban minorities, not the white middle class, were found to benefit most from a Catholic school education (Neal 1995).

Ironically, there is one circumstance in which opponents of school choice are likely to be proved right—when the number of choice schools is strictly limited. In this case, the most astute parents are likely to secure the small number of available places for their own children; other students will lack alternatives; and in the absence of meaningful competition, public schools will not be compelled to change. Since those who predict the failure of school choice generally push for strict limits on such plans, there is a danger that school choice will not receive a fair test. Opponents may ensure that choice is tried only under conditions likely to prove them right.

The point is an important one. An experiment may be so hedged in with restrictions that it fails to constitute a legitimate trial of market-based reform. The argument has been well expressed by Myron Lieberman in an analysis of the Milwaukee voucher plan. As implemented in 1990, the plan restricted participation to 1 percent of the Milwaukee public school enrollment. Eligible families' incomes could not exceed 175 percent of the poverty line. Voucher students could not comprise more than 49 percent of the students in any one school. Neither for-profit schools nor schools with a religious affiliation could participate. No extra funds were provided for learning-disabled or emotionally disturbed students, although participating schools were required to accept all voucher-carrying students. Finally, while the value of the voucher equalled barely half the per-pupil expenditure in Milwaukee public schools, participating voucher schools were not allowed to charge any tuition or fees in excess of the voucher.

Several features of this plan made it something less than a true test of competitive market forces. The scale was too small to encourage expansion of existing schools or new entries (since no school could come into being expressly to serve voucher students). The Milwaukee public schools had little to fear from a plan of this size. The schools with the best record of aiding urban minority populations—the parochial schools—were not allowed to participate. Participating schools were given half the per-pupil allotment of the public schools and were not allowed to charge more, even if both they and parents wanted the additional services that extra payments would make possible (Lieberman 1993).

These are not the only kind of restrictions placed on schools participating in choice plans. Under its charter school legislation, the State of Arizona appropriated just 1.6 million dollars for start-up costs in 46 charter schools, much less than what it spends to start a single public school (*New York Times*, March 6, 1996). As a consequence, charter schools have spent operating money on buildings rather than teachers or books. A variety of regulations severely restrict access to credit. Charter schools are not allowed to sell bonds. Since they are chartered for only five years, they have no access to long-term credit. And they are not considered to own assets like buildings and supplies, which cannot therefore be used as collateral for loans. Similar restrictions apply to charter schools in Minnesota. They are forbidden to use operating funds to purchase land or buildings. Yet they are not permitted to accept private or outside grants after their start-up period. No other public schools in the state are prevented by law from accepting corporate or foundation grants (Finn et al. 1996).

Numerous other restrictions have been placed on charter schools. Most states give local school boards control over charter schools, including the decision to issue a charter in the first place. In others, charter schools can be created only by converting an existing public school after a vote of staff (and in some cases, parents). Such requirements often result in protracted struggles to win approval of charters. Indeed, when asked how they would advise state legislators establishing guidelines for charter school creation, more respondents to the ECS-CSC survey mentioned school autonomy than start-up funds. Respondents recommended that charters be approved by some authority other than the local district, that local districts not be allowed to pressure charter schools into accepting various restrictive arrangements, and that charter schools not be bound by local labor-management agreements (Education Commission of the States and the Center for School Change 1995).

Like other market-based reforms, charter schools have been vigorously opposed by teachers' unions. Union opposition has been credited with helping to block charter school legislation in Illinois, Ohio, Connecticut, Washington, and Pennsylvania (Maus-Pugh 1995). The New Jersey Education Association has come out in support of a charter school bill that offers protection for school employees. Ballot referenda on educational vouchers have been defeated in Colorado and California; teachers unions and other associations of professional educators played key roles in these contests.

We do not mean to imply that all opposition to school choice is either self-interested or ill-considered. On the contrary, legitimate questions have been raised about school choice and other market-based reforms. Our argument is only that there should be no presumption that opponents are correct. Indeed, it is more than a little puzzling that a society that owes so much of its prosperity to a comparatively free market place should be so mistrustful of entrepreneurial activity in education. The evidence reviewed in this chapter suggests that when schools are freed from state regulation and forced to respond to market forces, personnel policies will change for the better. Given the potential that such reforms exhibit for attracting better teachers into the nation's classrooms, continued experimentation with school choice and privatization seems fully warranted. The greatest danger we foresee is that market forces will not be given a fair test, a danger compounded by the tendency of proponents to oversell the virtues of competition and promise more than can be achieved. In these circumstances, experimental trials of market-based reforms are only too likely to fail, a circumstance that will be used to discredit all such efforts.

NOTES

1. For a discussion of the pecuniary and nonpecuniary benefits of teacher unionism, see Everts and Stone (1984).

2. The private sector offers some in-kind benefits unavailable in most public schools, such as housing and meals for faculty and tuition waivers for their children. To some extent, these benefits compensate for lower salaries, though their importance is easily overstated. Only about 10 percent of the faculty in private schools receive tuition waivers at a point in time (McMillen, Rollefson, and Benson 1991). Housing (and to a lesser extent, meals) are usually provided to residence supervisors and therefore represent compensation for additional duties. Indeed, if all benefits are taken into account, public school teachers do better. Only three-quarters of private schools offer medical insurance to their teachers, compared to nearly all (96 percent) public schools. And while virtually all public school teachers are covered by a retirement plan, only 54 percent of private schools provide one.

3. A larger percentage of private school teachers graduated from colleges unrated by Barron's *Profiles*, though the implications for teacher quality are unclear. Many of these teachers graduated from Bible colleges and other little-known schools with a religious affiliation. These colleges have evidently chosen not to provide information to Barron's editors, possibly because they do not wish to broaden their applicant base.

4. Most of them teach in the early grades. Fewer than one-half of these instructors have any students above third grade, and fewer than 16 percent teach any high school classes, even subjects like art and music.

5. It may be objected that "excellent" does not mean the same thing in the public and private sectors, perhaps because the job of a public school teacher is more difficult. These intersectoral differences remain, however, after controlling for a variety of school and community characteristics. Even if a comparison of absolute responses is felt to be questionable, it is revealing that pri-

vate school heads rate their experienced teachers higher relative to new instructors than do public school principals. Thus, it appears the private sector does a better job of staff development and selectively retaining the best teachers. Further discussion of these data appears in Ballou and Podgursky (1995b).

6. There is also a widespread perception that class sizes are smaller in the private sector. In fact, the differences are slight, with private school classes smaller by only one or two students, on average.

7. The possible responses to each item were "strongly agree," "somewhat agree," "somewhat disagree," and strongly disagree." On virtually all items, a majority of teachers expressed agreement (or, if the item was worded negatively, disagreement). Thus the most important difference was whether they agreed strongly or with reservations.

8. A strong egalitarian ethos in many religious schools appears to discourage the use of incentive pay. Some administrators have expressed particular concern that differentials based on performance would threaten the staff's sense of community and shared purpose. On the other hand, the practices of these schools might be different if there were not a much larger public sector setting compensation on the basis of teachers' education and experience. It is likely that public sector policies establish professional norms from which private schools find it difficult to deviate. Performance-based compensation might be more widespread if education were wholly conducted by private schools competing in the market place.

9. For example, despite a formal confidentiality agreement between the Lebanon, Connecticut school district and the teacher's association, a list of awardees' names was circulated (apparently by unhappy teachers), causing problems with parents and teachers and contributing to the eventual termination of the merit pay plan (Hatry, Greiner, and Ashford 1994).

10. This also causes problems for administrators. Publishing the names of recognized "master teachers" has sometimes resulted in conflict between principals and parents when the latter insist that their children be taught by these instructors (Hatry and Greiner 1985).

11. Administrators of religious schools, on the other hand, are much more likely to respond that they value or even require certification. The reason, however, is revealing. Certified teachers enhance the school's legitimacy in the eyes of the public or regional accrediting boards, i.e., the school meets "all the requirements that public schools have to meet." Pedagogical concerns have rarely been mentioned.

12. It is instructive to contrast programs of this type with one of the largest, most highly publicized mentor plans in the public schools, the California mentor teacher program. On paper the California plan looks promising: mentor teachers are paid an extra $4,000 annually and are provided release time for their extra duties. Through discussions with California educators we have learned, however, that no provision is made to reduce teachers' work loads on a regular basis (say, by one course). Teachers seeking release time must prepare lesson plans for a substitute, a task regarded as sufficiently onerous that many mentors choose to carry out their mentoring activities after school rather than during regular school hours. Perhaps partly as a result, mentoring has come to mean something other than supervision and help for beginning teachers. Instead, many mentors prepare plans to update or otherwise modify the school's curriculum or to introduce other pedagogical innovations. The final decision to implement these plans rests with the administrator, who may not adopt them.

13. Probationary teachers are generally entitled to some due process. Timely notice of nonrenewal must be provided. In addition, fourteen states grant probationary teachers the right to a hearing before dismissal. However, except when nonrenewal occurs on ground that infringe individual liberty or when probationary teachers have established some property right in their jobs (an unusual event), contract renewal is a matter of board discretion. No advance hearings or statement of reasons is required (Valente 1987).

14. It is interesting that even in those Catholic archdioceses where teachers are represented by unions, contracts often provide less protection for senior teachers than in the public sector. Thus, in one Massachusetts archdiocese, seven factors are used to determine who is to be laid off. Only if two teachers are equal on the other six does seniority prove decisive. These other factors include annual performance evaluations and ability to teach multiple subjects. Moreover, senior teachers are not allowed to bump instructors in other buildings, significantly limiting the damage that can be done.

15. Many of those laid off do not, in fact, find other teaching jobs, as an analysis of data from the Teacher Follow-Up survey to the 1987-88 SASS shows. Of the 13 percent of the private school workforce that left teaching after the 1987-88 school year, 7 percent indicated that their reason was a school staffing action rather than personal choice (Choy et al. 1992). Thus, .9 percent of the private sector workforce (.13 x .07) was essentially forced out through layoffs.

16. These are not the only objections to school choice. Rural areas will likely be underserved (though innovations in distance learning improve prospects for delivering services to areas of low population density). In many communities, transportation costs may limit the extent of the market and the amount of choice available to parents. Others have raised concerns about the transmission of values appropriate to a democratic, pluralistic polity (Levin 1989; Hawley 1996). As noted in the previous chapter, however, there is much disagreement about the values public schools should impart. Many would dispute the claim that graduates of public as opposed to private schools exhibit more public virtues or become better citizens (Lieberman 1993).

Appendix 6A
Public and Private School Salary Regressions

The Model

The dependent variable is the natural logarithm of base pay plus bonuses. Bonuses represent additional pay for performance of regular duties. This excludes extra compensation received for doing extra work (e.g., coaching, summer school).

The independent variables in the model fall into four categories: (1) a teacher's education and experience; (2) overall measures of salary in the district (or at the school); (3) in-kind compensation and religious affiliation (for private school teachers); (4) performance incentives.

Teacher's education and experience

There are five levels of education: less than a bachelor's degree, bachelor's degree, master's degree, special certificate (e.g., 6th year certificate), and doctoral degree. The bachelor's degree is the omitted category. The others enter the model as dummy variables, except for master's degree, which is interacted with the salary increment (premium) awarded teachers with a master's degree, as explained below.

There are three measures of experience: full-time public school experience, full-time private school experience, and prior part-time experience. For public school teachers, their full-time public school experience is interacted with a measure of the salary increment (premium) that their current districts pay for experience, as explained below. A similar measure is constructed for private school teachers' experience within that sector. Full-time experience outside the current sector and part-time experience enter the equation simply as the number of years in question.

School's pay level

The 1990-91 SASS furnishes three variables measuring the overall level of salaries in the district (or private school): (1) starting salary offered teachers with a bachelor's degree and no prior experience; (2) starting salary offered teachers with a master's degree and no prior experience; (3) salary offered teachers with a master's degree and twenty years' experience. The difference (2) - (1) (in logs) measures the premium on a master's degree and is interacted with a binary variable indicating whether the teacher holds a master's degree. We obtain the returns to experience by assuming equal percentage increases for each year of experience. We also assume a teacher reaches the top of the salary schedule after twenty years. The annual premium on experience is therefore computed as the difference (3) - (2) (in logs), divided by twenty. The censored measure of experience is the maximum of within-sector experience and 20, and is interacted with the premium on experience.

Thus, we have three controls for the salary schedule used by the district (or private school). The first is starting pay for teachers with bachelor's degrees. The second is a measure of the extra compensation the district pays to teachers with a master's degree. The third is a measure of the increment to experience times a given teacher's within-sector experience. To the extent that teachers do not receive full credit for prior experience in other districts, the coefficient on the third variable will be less than one. On the other hand, the imputed return to holding a master's degree will be too small if schedules fan out with experience (i.e., experienced instructors obtain a larger percentage increase in pay when they obtain a master's degree). In this case, the coefficient on the MA variable will exceed one (to compensate). There are other nonlinearities in schedules, so that our model will, at best, only approximate schedules in actual use.

In-kind compensation and religious school indicators

There are three measures of in-kind compensation: housing, meals, and tuition (for faculty children). Unfortunately, the SASS reports only whether a teacher receives each form of compensation, not the dollar value. Thus, each enters as a binary indicator. In the private school equation, we use also include two dummy variables indicating whether the school is Catholic or of another religious affiliation. Different intercepts capture the degree to which different types of schools might deviate from their stated policy. Such deviations are common. As explained in chapter 6, Catholic parishes often set salaries in their grammar schools at a lower level than recommended by the diocesan schedule.

Performance-related bonuses

There are four incentives: (1) serving as a mentor/master teacher; (2) teaching in a shortage field (e.g., math or science); (3) teaching in an undesirable location (e.g., inner city school); (4) merit pay. Since these are intradistrict bonuses, the undesirable location premium is defined only for public schools (since most private schools are their own district and have only one location). Being a mentor/master teacher may involve extra duties, so that to some extent the extra pay is for extra work.

Awards may be given as cash bonuses, as advances on the salary schedule, or in other unspecified forms. Unfortunately, the data do not include the magnitude of these awards. Only binary indicators are available. Thus, the coefficient on a binary indicator for merit pay recipients becomes an estimate of the average size of a merit award (as a percentage of pay).

In fact, the situation is somewhat more complicated than this. There are two relevant binary variables for each type of incentive. The first indicates whether the school offers such a bonus (e.g., has a merit pay plan). The second indicates whether the teacher "receives the incentive." Presumably this means the teacher is receiving a bonus, not simply that the teacher is a participant in the plan (and therefore responding to the incentive). However, there may be teachers who gave the question the latter interpretation.

In addition, there are some discrepancies in the way these variables are defined at the school level and at the teacher level. For example, the school is asked "Is there a formal program to help beginning teachers (such as a master or mentor teacher program) in use in this school?" The teacher is asked whether he or she receives the following pay incentive: "additional pay for assuming additional responsibilities as a master or mentor teacher (e.g., supervising new teachers)." Ambiguity arises because some schools may assign teachers to help new instructors without calling them mentors or master teachers, and because some schools with master or mentor teacher programs assign them duties other than supervision of new teachers (e.g., curriculum development).

Ambiguities also arise with respect to the other incentive plans. Schools (or districts) are asked whether they have a plan, questions that either explicitly or implicitly refer to the current year. Teachers are asked whether they receive such an incentive. Thus, a teacher hired in a shortage field who was advanced on the salary schedule at the time of hire would presumably indicate (even several years later) that he was receiving the incentive, since it had been built into his base. But if the school had subsequently discontinued the policy, it would indicate that it had no such plan. Similar discrepancies could arise for merit pay if a teacher was receiving a merit bonus for performance the previous year, but the plan itself had been discontinued (not an uncommon event).

These distinctions are of some importance, since there are, in fact, many discrepancies between the answers given by schools and by the teachers who work in them. Many teachers claiming to receive these incentives are employed in schools that say they do not offer them. These discrepancies may be the result of coding errors or mistakes either on the teacher's part or the part of the district office, or they may represent accurate responses which differ for the reasons stated above. Due to these ambiguities, we introduce three sets of variables capturing the effect of incentive plans on a teacher's pay.

First, for each incentive we introduce a dummy variable indicating whether the district or school has a plan or policy of that type. Note that this variable applies to all teachers at that school, not just those who receive the bonus. This is a background control for any factors that cause such schools to deviate from what the model would otherwise predict salaries to be. Thus, our estimate of the average size of a bonus does not pick up mere school effects.

Second, we include a dummy variable indicating whether the teacher reports receiving the incentive. And third, we interact this indicator with the first, giving us a dummy variable for those teachers who say they receive the incentive from districts that say they offer it. The average bonus for these recipients will be the sum of the coefficients on the second and third dummy variables (for each incentive plan). The average bonus (if that is what it is) for recipients in schools that do not offer these plans is the coefficient on the second indicator variable.

Data

Data were obtained from the 1990-91 Schools and Staffing Survey. Separate estimates were obtained for public and for private schools. Among the latter, only schools that used a salary schedule were retained in the estimation sample. (Those that did not answered a slightly different set of questions. It is possible to overlook the differences and pool the two sets of private schools by making some adjustments to variable definitions; when this is done, very similar results are obtained).

Only full-time teachers were used, excluding both part-time employees and teachers with part-time administrative responsibilities. Unpaid volunteers were dropped. All remaining teachers earned annual salaries of at least $5,000. The private school sample also excludes teachers who are members of religious orders, whose compensation is often not market-based.

Because the model combines variables from different components of the survey, teachers whose schools or districts failed to respond to the survey were also dropped from the estimation sample.

Results

Results are presented in appendix table 6A.1. The coefficients on incentive variables are frequently insignificant in the public sector equations. Some of those that are significant have a perverse sign (e.g., teaching in an undesirable location). The average merit pay bonus is about 2 percent of pay. Mentor teachers receive even less, about 1 percent. (When the dependent variable is defined to include extra pay received for extra duties during the school year, the coefficient on mentoring rises to about 2 percent. Other incentive coefficients are not affected.)

In the private sector, incentives are larger and more consistently significant, despite the smaller sample size. Merit pay increases salaries by nearly 12 percent on average. Mentor teachers earn an extra 4 percent. (When the dependent variable includes extra pay for extra duties, these coefficients rise to 14 percent and 5 percent, respectively.) In both the public and private sectors, bonuses for teaching in a shortage field are either very small (<2 percent) or estimated so imprecisely that they fail conventional significance tests.

We have also reestimated the model deleting the binary indicators for teachers who claimed to receive incentives in schools that did not offer them; i.e. we assumed such responses were errors and coded these persons as non-recipients. Results were virtually identical to those obtained above.

162

Appendix Table 6A.1. Salary Regressions

Dependent variable: log of base pay plus bonuses	Public	Private
Starting pay	1.062 (.015)	.824 (.030)
Catholic school	----	-.062 (.015)
Other religious school	----	-.078 (.017)
No bachelor's degree	.076 (.011)	-.230(.050)
Premium for master's x MA	1.091 (.030)	.756 (.105)
Special certificate (e.g., sixth year)	.034 (.007)	.022 (.022)
Doctoral degree	.080 (.014)	.137 (.040)
Premium for experience x experience ≤20	.916 (.005)	.861 (.033)
Prior public school experience	----	.007 (.001)
Prior private school experience	.006 (.001)	----
Prior part-time experience	.007 (.001)	.007 (.002)
Teacher receives housing	----	-.004 (.036)
Teacher receives meals	----	.015 (.019)
Teacher receives tuition reduction	----	.005 (.012)
School has mentor plan	-.003 (.004)	.001 (.008)
School has merit pay plan	-.020 (.003)	.014 (.014)
School pays for undesirable location	.005 (.027)	----
School pays for shortage fields	-.015 (.005)	.016 (.015)
Teacher receives mentor pay	.013 (.007)	.019 (.022)
Teacher receives shortage pay	-.000 (.013)	.083 (.061)
Teacher receives location pay	.011 (.050)	----
Teacher receives merit pay	-.024 (.009)	.010 (.027)
Mentor pay: receives x school has plan	-.006 (.008)	.018 (.020)
Shortage pay: receives x school has plan	.007 (.006)	.166 (.377)
Location pay: receives x school has plan	-.068 (.050)	----
Merit pay: receives x school has plan	.043 (.012)	.092 (.025)
R-squared	.75	.68
Regression MSE	.021	.039
Number of observations	38,069	3,576

SOURCE: Schools and Staffing Survey, 1990-91.

CHAPTER 7

Conclusion

The argument of this book can be summarized in the following five propositions.

1. Higher teacher salaries have had little if any discernible impact on the quality of newly recruited teachers.

Using such indicators as the quality of the college from which teachers graduated and the degree of difficulty and rigor in their undergraduate major, we find essentially no relationship between salary growth and the qualifications of new teachers compared to experienced teachers in the same state. We have put the data through a variety of tests to see whether our negative findings might be due to various biases. None of these tests has changed our conclusion. While it remains possible that weaknesses in the data or faulty analytical techniques have caused us to miss improvement that took place, it seems surprising that a response to higher pay would be so difficult to detect, and that there would be no obvious connection between the amount teacher pay rose and the improvement in the quality of a state's new teachers.

2. The failure of this policy can be traced, in part, to structural features of the teacher labor market.

Teacher salaries are not differentiated on the basis of performance. When teacher pay rises, it rises for all teachers. As a result, quit rates fall and jobs become more difficult to find. The fact that prospective teachers must invest in occupation-specific training that has no value outside public education makes them sensitive to declining job prospects. This effect is greatest for those with the most attractive options outside teaching, who incur the greatest loss if they train to become teachers and cannot find a teaching job. By contrast, persons with no professional prospects outside education will scarcely be deterred by a decline in job opportunities.

3. Recruitment of better teachers is further impeded by the fact that public schools show no preference for applicants who have strong academic records.

Even a declining job market might not discourage bright applicants from pursuing teaching careers if they could be confident that their chances of obtaining jobs remained good. Unfortunately, there seem to be no grounds for such confidence. Public schools are no more likely to hire these candidates than those with far weaker academic records.

4. A variety of reforms have been proposed that might lower entry barriers and improve job prospects of more capable prospective teachers.

Differentiating salaries on the basis of performance (or measured competencies) could provide encouragement to better teachers without stimulating a general increase in teacher supply. Licensing requirements could be relaxed, particularly for individuals who demonstrate promise in other ways. Standards could be raised for teachers or, alternatively, for students, leading schools to value instructors with stronger cognitive skills. Teacher tenure and other job protections could be weakened, making it easier for administrators to dismiss ineffective teachers. Such reforms face a host of practical and political difficulties, not least the opposition of powerful entrenched interests that benefit from the way teachers are currently trained, licensed, and employed.

5. To judge from the practices of private schools, market-based reforms would improve the quality of the teaching work force.

Private schools place more emphasis on academics and the recruitment of faculty who have strong academic records. They are more likely to differentiate salaries on the basis of performance and to dismiss ineffective teachers. While there remain many unanswered questions about school choice, the record so far would seem to encourage further experimentation. Entrepreneurs appear ready to provide services to a wide variety of students, not just the most affluent or advantaged. Unfortunately, opposition to market-based reforms is intense. This opposition has influenced charter school legislation and the design of other choice plans, with the unfortunate consequence that market-based reform may not receive a fair trial.

It is customary at the conclusion of a work of this kind for the authors to present their policy recommendations, a set of proposals that would, in their view, correct the problems they have been at pains to identify. We offer no such list. There are a great many proposals on the table already. Instead, we close by highlighting those reforms now underway that seem to offer the best opportunity of improving the way the teacher labor market functions.

On the supply side of the market, licensing requirements should be relaxed so that promising applicants can seek jobs without first investing a year in the acquisition of a credential they may never use or use only a short while. This policy is already a feature of alternative certification programs established to recruit minority teachers and instructors in shortage areas. Many private schools that prefer their teachers to be certified also hire instructors who lack this credential, allowing them to complete the necessary course work once they have started teaching. Induction and internship programs provide on-the-job assistance to beginning teachers. Given that such policies are widely and successfully followed in the private sector, we see no justification for current licensing requirements. At a minimum, alternative certification programs should be expanded to serve the more general purpose of recruiting better teachers all around.

Still, such changes may not accomplish much if school districts continue to prefer applicants with traditional training and to overlook non-education majors with strong academic backgrounds. Altering behavior on the demand side of the market will require more radical reforms. For reasons detailed in chapter 5, we are skeptical that current efforts to enhance public schools' accountability will have much effect on the way teaching applicants are screened. We are more optimistic about reforms—like the charter school movement—that create schools that must compete for students, run by entrepreneurs less likely to be bound by traditional views. Unfortunately, reforms attempting to create a competitive market in educational services are strongly opposed by vested interests within the professional education community, raising the possibility that charter schools will become isolated pockets of quality while business goes on as usual in the schools attended by the great majority of the nation's children.

References

Akerlof, George A. 1970. "The Market for Lemons," *Quarterly Journal of Economics* 84, 3 (August): 488-500.

Antos, Joseph R., and Sherwin Rosen. 1975. "Discrimination in the Market for Public School Teachers," *Journal of Econometrics* 3, 2 (May): 123-150.

Ballou, Dale. 1996. "Do Public Schools Hire the Best Applicants?" *Quarterly Journal of Economics* 111, 1 (February): 97-134.

Ballou, Dale, and Michael Podgursky. 1993a. "Have Higher Salaries Improved Teacher Quality?" Amherst, MA: University of Massachusetts, unpublished.

_____. 1993b. "Teachers' Attitudes Toward Merit Pay: Examining Conventional Wisdom," *Industrial and Labor Relations Review* 47, 1 (October): 50-61.

_____. 1995a. "Education Policy and Teacher Effort," *Industrial Relations* 34, 1 (January): 21-39.

_____. 1995b. "How Principals Rate Their Teachers: Implications for Personnel Policy in Public and Private Schools." Amherst, MA: University of Massachusetts, unpublished.

_____. 1995c. "The Private Market Value of Teacher Certification." Amherst, MA: University of Massachusetts, unpublished.

_____. 1995d. "Recruiting Smarter Teachers," *Journal of Human Resources* 30, 2 (Spring): 326-338.

Barro, Stephen M. 1992. "Models for Projecting Teacher Supply, Demand, and Quality: An Assessment of the State of the Art." In *Teacher Supply, Demand, and Quality*, Erling E. Boe and Dorothy M. Gilford eds. Washington, DC: National Academy Press.

Barron's Profiles of American Colleges. 1991. 18th Edition. New York: Barron's Educational Services.

Beales, Janet R. 1994. *Teacher, Inc.: A Private-Practice Option for Educators*. Los Angeles: Reason Foundation.

Beaudin, Barbara. 1991-92. "Update on Newly Hired Connecticut Public School Educators: September 1990." Hartford, CT: Connecticut State Department of Education.

_____. 1993-94. "Newly Hired Connecticut Public School Educators: September 1992." Hartford, CT: Connecticut State Department of Education.

_____. 1994-95. "Teacher Supply and Demand in Connecticut: A Summary of Ten Years of State Level Research." Hartford, CT: Connecticut State Department of Education.

Bigler, Philip, and Karen Lockard. 1992. *Failing Grades: A Teacher's Report Card on Education in America*. Arlington, VA: Vandamere.

Bishop, John. 1993. "What's Wrong With American Secondary Schools?" In *The Economic Consequences of American Education*, Robert Thornton and Richard Aronson, eds. Greenwich, CT: JAI Press.

_____. 1994. "Signalling, Incentives, and School Organization in France, the Netherlands, Britain and the United States: Lessons for Education Economics." Working Paper #94-25, Center for Advanced Human Resource Studies, Cornell University.

Bok, Derek. 1993. *The Cost of Talent*. New York: Free Press.

Bowles, Samuel, and Henry M. Levin. 1968. "The Determinants of Scholastic Achievement: An Appraisal of Some Recent Evidence," *Journal of Human Resources* 3, 1 (Winter): 3-24.

Boyer, Ernest L. 1983. *High School: A Report on Secondary Education in America*. New York: Harper & Row.

Brandt, Richard M. 1990. *Incentive Pay and Career Ladders for Today's Teachers*. Albany: State University of New York.

Bridges, Edwin M. 1992. *The Incompetent Teacher: The Challenge and the Response*. Philadelphia: Falmer Press.

Bryk, Anthony S., and Valerie E. Lee. 1993. "Lessons from Catholic High Schools on Renewing Our Educational Institutions." Reprinted in *Network News and Views*. Indianapolis, IN: Educational Excellence Network.

Burks, Mary Paxton. 1987. *Requirements for Certification for Elementary Schools, Secondary Schools, Junior Colleges*. Chicago: University of Chicago Press.

Carnegie Foundation for the Advancement of Teaching. 1985. *The Condition of Teaching*. Princeton, NJ: Carnegie Foundation for the Advancement of Teaching.

Carnegie Forum on Education and the Economy. Task Force on Teaching as a Profession. 1986. *A Nation Prepared: Teachers for the 21st Century*. New York: Carnegie Corporation.

Chambers, Jay G. 1985. "Patterns of Compensation of Public and Private School Teachers," *Economics of Education Review* 4, 4: 291-310.

Childs, Ruth A., and Lawrence Rudner. 1990. *States' Testing of Teachers: The 1990 Report*. Washington DC: American Institute for Research.

Choy, Susan P., et al. 1992. *Schools and Staffing the United States: A Statistical Profile, 1987-88*. Washington, DC: U.S. Department of Education, National Center for Education Statistics.

_____. 1993. *America's Teachers: Profile of a Profession*. Washington DC: U.S. Department of Education, National Center for Education Statistics.

Chubb, John E., and Eric Al Hanushek. 1990. "Reforming Education Reform." In *Setting National Priorities*, Henry J. Aaron, ed. Washington, DC: Brookings.

Coleman, James, et. al. 1966. *Equality of Educational Opportunity.* Washington DC: U.S. Government Printing Office.

_____. 1982. "Cognitive Outcomes in Public and Private Schools." *Sociology of Education* 55 (April/July): 65-76.

Coleman, James S., and Thomas Hoffer. 1987. *Public and Private High Schools: The Impact of Communities.* New York: Basic Books.

College Entrance Examination Board. 1980. *National College-Bound Seniors, 1980.* Princeton NJ: College Entrance Examination Board.

_____. 1992. *College-Bound Seniors, National Report; 1992 Profile of SAT and Achievement Test Takers.* Princeton NJ: College Entrance Examination Board.

College Placement Council. 1994. *CPC Salary Survey.* Bethlehem, PA: College Placement Council.

Committee for Economic Development. 1985. Research and Policy Committee. *Investing in Our Children: Business and the Public Schools.* New York: Committee for Economic Development.

Corme, Michael A., Barry T. Hirsch, and David A. MacPherson. 1990. "Union Membership and Coverage in the US, 1983-1988," *Industrial and Labor Relations Review* 44, 1 (October): 5-33.

Cornett, Lynne M. 1987. *More Pay for Teachers and Administrators Who Do More: Incentive Pay Programs.* Atlanta, GA: Southern Regional Education Board.

_____. 1991. *Linking Performance to Rewards for Teachers, Principals, and Schools.* Atlanta, GA: Southern Regional Education Board.

Cornett, Lynn M. and Gale F. Gaines. 1992. *Focusing on Student Outcomes: Roles for Incentive Programs.* Atlanta: Southern Regional Education Board.

Cramer, Jerome. 1983. "Yes—Merit Pay Can Be a Horror, but a Few School Systems Have Done It Right," *American School Board Journal* 170, 9 (September): 28-34.

Darling-Hammond, Linda. 1984. *Beyond the Commission Reports: The Coming Crisis in Teaching.* Santa Monica: RAND.

_____. 1994. "Who Will Speak for the Children? How 'Teach for America' Hurts Urban Schools and Students," *Phi Delta Kappan* 76, 1 (September): 21-34.

Dworkin, A. Gerald. 1987. *Teacher Burnout in the Public Schools.* Albany: State University of New York Press.

Eberts, Randall W., and Joe A. Stone. 1984. *Unions and Public Schools.* Lexington, MA: D.C. Heath.

Education Commission of the States and the Center for School Change. 1995. *Preliminary Results from a Survey of Approved Charter Schools.* Denver, CO: Education Commission of the States.

Educational Testing Service. 1992. *Guidelines for Proper Use of the Praxis Series: Professional Assessments for Beginning Teachers.* Princeton, NJ: ETS.

Ehrenberg, Ronald G., and Dominic J. Brewer. 1993. "Did Teachers' Race and Verbal Ability Matter in the 1960's? *Coleman* Revisited." NBER Working Paper No. 4293.

_____. 1994. "Do School and Teacher Characteristics Matter? Evidence from High School and Beyond," *Economics of Education Review* 13, 1: 1-17.

Elam, Stanley M. 1989. "The Second Gallup/Phi Delta Kappa Poll of Teachers' Attitudes Toward the Public Schools," *Phi Delta Kappan* 70, 10 (June): 785-90.

Farber, Barry A. 1991. *Crisis in Education: Stress and Burnout in the American Teacher.* San Francisco: Jossey-Bass.

Feistritzer, C. Emily. 1990. *Profile of Teachers in the U.S.—1990.* Washington, DC: National Center for Education Information.

Feistritzer, C. Emily, and David T. Chester. 1993. *Alternative Teacher Certification: A State-by-State Analysis 1993-94.* Washington DC: National Center for Education Information.

Ferguson, Ronald F. 1991. "Paying for Public Education: New Evidence on How and Why Money Matters." *Harvard Journal on Legislation* 28: 465-498.

Finn, Chester E. Jr. 1991. *We Must Take Charge: Our Schools and Our Future.* New York: Free Press.

Finn, Chester E., et al. 1996. *Charter Schools in Action: A First Look.* Washington DC: Hudson Institute.

Flyer, Frederick, and Sherwin Rosen. 1996. "Some Economics of Precollege Teaching." In *Assessing Educational Practice: The Contribution of Economists*, William E. Becker and William J. Baumol, eds. Cambridge, MA: MIT Press.

Frankel, Martin, and Peter Stowe. 1990. *New Teachers in the Job Market, 1987 Update.* Washington, DC: U.S. Department of Education.

Galambos, Eva C. 1985. *Teacher Preparation: The Anatomy of a College Degree.* Atlanta: Southern Regional Education Board.

Gallup, A. 1984. "The Gallop Poll of Teachers' Attitudes Toward the Public Schools," *Phi Delta Kappan* 66, 2 (October): 97-107.

Attrition

Gilford, Dorothy M., and Ellen Tenenbaum, eds. 1990. *Precollege Science and Mathematics Teachers: Monitoring Supply, Demand and Quality.* Washington, DC: National Academy Press.

Haney, Walter, et al. 1987. "Charms Talismanic: Testing Teachers for the Improvement of American Education." In *Review of Research in Education,* Vol. 14, Ernst Z. Rothkopf, ed. Washington DC: American Educational Research Association.

Hanushek, Eric A. 1970. "The Production of Education, Teacher Quality, and Efficiency." In *Do Teachers Make a Difference?* Washington, DC: U.S. Department of Health, Education and Welfare.

_____. 1971. "Teacher Characteristics and Gains in Student Achievement: Estimation Using Micro Data," *American Economic Review* 61, 2 (May): 280-88.

_____. 1981. "Throwing Money at Schools," *Journal of Policy Analysis and Management* 1, 1 (Fall): 19-42.

_____. 1986. "The Economics of Schooling: Production and Efficiency in Public Schools," *Journal of Economic Literature* 24, 3 (September): 1141-1177.

Hanushek, Eric A., and Richard R. Pace. 1995. "Who Chooses to Teach (and Why)?" *Economics of Education Review* 14, 2: 101-117.

Hanushek, Eric A., Steven G. Rivkin, and Dean T. Jamison. 1992. "Improving Educational Outcomes While Controlling Cost." Carnegie-Rochester Conference Series on Public Policy, No. 37.

Hatry, Harry P., John M. Greiner, and Brenda G. Ashford. 1994. *Issues and Case Studies in Teacher Incentive Plans.* Washington, DC: Urban Institute.

Hatry, Harry P., and John H. Greiner. 1985. *Issues and Case Studies in Teacher incentive Plans,* Washington, DC: Urban Institute Press.

Hawley, Willis D. 1996. "The Predictable Consequences of School Choice," *Education Week* (April 10): 56.

The Holmes Group. 1986. *Tomorrow's Teachers.* East Lansing, MI: Holmes Group.

Hood, Stafford, and Lawrence Parker. 1991. "Minorities, Teacher Testing, and Recent U.S. Supreme Court Holdings: A Regressive Step," *Teachers College Record* 92, 4 (Summer): 603-618.

Jacobson, Stephen L. 1988. "The Distribution of Salary Increments and Its Effect on Teacher Retention," *Educational Administration Quarterly* 24, 2 (May): 178-199.

James, Estelle, et al. 1989. "College Quality and Future Earnings: Where Should You Send Your Child to College?" *American Economic Review* (May): 247-252.

Johnson, Susan Moore. 1990. *Teachers at Work: Achieving Success in Our Schools*. New York: Basic Books.

Kirst, Michael W., and Carolyn Kelley. 1993. "Positive Impacts of Reform Efforts in the 1980's." Presentation at University of California at Berkeley symposium, "A Nation at Risk Ten Years Later," April 8, 1993.

Koerner, James D. 1963. *The Miseducation of American Teachers*. Cambridge, MA: Riverside Press.

Kopp, Wendy. 1992. "Reforming Schools of Education Will Not Be Enough," *Yale Law and Policy Review* 10, 1 (November): 58-68.

Kramer, Rita. 1991. *Ed School Follies*. New York: Macmillan.

Lankford, Hamilton, and James Wyckoff. 1994. "Which Teachers Received Real Salary Increases in New York, 1970-94?" Presented at the Summer Data Conference of the National Center for Education Statistics, July 27-20.

Leetsma, Robert, et al. 1987. "A Report from the U.S. Study of Education in Japan." Washington, DC: Government Printing Office.

Levin, Henry M. 1989. "Education as a Public and Private Good." In *Public Values, Private Schools*, Neal E. Devens. ed. New York: Falmer Press.

_____. 1993. "The Economics of Education for At-Risk Students." In *Essays on the Economics of Education*, Emily P. Hoffman, ed. Kalamazoo, MI: W.E. Upjohn Institute for Employment Research.

Lieberman, Myron. 1986. "Are Teachers Underpaid?" *The Public Interest*, 84 (Summer): 12-28.

_____. 1993. *Public Education: An Autopsy*. Cambridge, MA: Harvard University Press.

Lindsay, Drew. 1996. "Critics Target Teacher Tenure, But Most Blows Miss Mark," *Education Week* (April 17): 11-13.

Lortie, Dan C. 1975. *Schoolteacher*. Chicago: University of Chicago Press.

Lutz, Frank W., and Jerry B. Hutton. 1989. "Alternative Teacher Certification: Its Policy Implications for Classroom and Personnel Practice," *Education Evaluation and Policy Analysis* 11, 3 (Fall): 237-254.

Manski, Charles F. 1987. "Academic Ability, Earnings, and the Decision to Become a Teacher: Evidence from the National Longitudinal Study of the High School Class of 1972" In *Public Sector Payrolls,* David A. Wise, ed. Chicago: University of Chicago Press.

Maus-Pugh, Thomas. 1995. "Charter Schools 1995: A Survey and Analysis of the Laws and Practices of the States," *Education Policy Analysis Archives* 3, 13 (July 12). Available at http://elam.ed.asu.edu/epoal.

McGrath, Mary Jo. 1993. "When It's Time to Dismiss an Incompetent Teacher." Reprinted in *Network News and Views*, May. Indianapolis, IN: Educational Excellence Network.

McLaughlin, John M. 1995. "Public Education and Private Enterprise: Where's This New Relationship Going?" *The School Administrator* 52, 7 (August): 7-13.

McMahon, Walter W., and Shao-Chung Chang. 1991. *Geographical Cost of Living Differences: Interstate and Intrastate, Update 1991.* Normal, IL: Center for the Study of Educational Finance, Illinois State University.

McMillen, Marilyn, Mary Rollefson, and Peter Benson. 1991. *Detailed Characteristics of Private Schools and Staff: 1987-88.* Washington, DC: United States Department of Education, Office of Educational Research and Improvement.

Milkovich, George, and Jerry Newman. 1993. *Compensation.* Homewood, IL: Irwin.

Milkovich, George, and Alexandra K. Wigdor, eds. 1991. *Pay for Performance: Evaluating Performance Appraisal and Merit Pay.* Washington, DC: National Academy Press.

Monk, David H. 1994. "Subject Area Preparation of Secondary Mathematics and Science Teachers and Student Achievement," *Economics of Education Review* 13, 2: 125-145.

Mont, Daniel, and Daniel I. Rees. 1996. "The Influence of Classroom Characteristics on High School Teacher Turnover," *Economic Inquiry* 34 (January): 152-167.

Murnane, Richard J. 1983. "Understanding the Sources of Teaching Competence: Choices, Skills, and the Limits of Training," *Teachers College Record* 84, 3 (Spring): 564-569.

_____. 1986. "Comparisons of Private and Public Schools: The Critical Role of Regulations." In *Private Education: Studies in Choice and Public Policy,* Daniel C. Levy, ed. Oxford: Oxford University Press.

Murnane, Richard J., et al. 1987. "Changes in Teacher Salaries During the 1970's: The Role of School District Demographics," *Economics of Education Review* 6, 4: 379-388.

_____. 1991. *Who Will Teach? Policies that Matter.* Cambridge, MA: Harvard University Press.

Murnane, Richard J., and David K. Cohen. 1986. "Merit Pay and the Evaluation Problem: Why Most Merit Pay Plans Fail and a Few Survive," *Harvard Educational Review* 56, 1 (February): 1-17.

Murnane, Richard J., and Randall J. Olsen. 1990. "The Effects of Salaries and Opportunity Costs on Length of Stay in Teaching: Evidence from North Carolina," *Journal of Human Resources* 25, 1 (Winter): 106-124.

Murnane, Richard J., and Michael Schwinden. 1989. "Race, Gender, and Opportunity: Supply and Demand for New Teachers in North Carolina,

1975-1985," *Educational Evaluation and Policy Analysis* 11, 2 (Summer): 93-108.

Nathan, Joe. 1995. "Charter Public Schools: A Brief History and Preliminary Lessons." University of Minnesota, Hubert H. Humphrey Institute of Public Affairs, March.

National Association of State Directors of Teacher Education and Certification (NASDTEC). 1991. *Manual on Certification and Preparation of Educational Personnel in the United States.* Dubuque, IA: Kendall/Hunt.

National Commission on Excellence in Education. 1983. *A Nation at Risk: The Imperative for Educational Reform.* Washington, DC: Government Printing Office.

National Education Association. 1982. *N.E.A. Handbook, 1982-83.* Washington, DC. NEA.

_____. 1987. *Status of the American Public School Teacher, 1985-86.* Washington, DC: NEA.

_____. 1992. *Status of the American Public School Teacher 1990-1991.* Washington, DC: NEA.

National Scholarship Center. 1995. *Just Doing It 2: 1995 Annual Survey of The Private Voucher Movement in America.* Washington, DC: National Scholarship Center.

National School Boards Association. 1995. *Private Options for Public Schools: Ways Public Schools Are Exploring Privatization.* Alexandria, VA: NSBA.

National Science Board Commission on Precollege Education in Mathematics, Science and Technology. 1983. *Educating Americans for the 21st Century.* Washington DC: National Science Foundation.

Neal, Derek. 1995. "The Effect of Catholic Secondary Schooling on Educational Attainment." NBER Working Paper No. 5353.

Nelson, F. Howard. 1985. "New Perspectives on the Teacher Quality Debate: Empirical Evidence from the National Longitudinal Study," *Journal of Educational Research* 78, 3 (January/February): 133-140.

New Jersey State Department of Education. 1991. *The New Jersey Provisional Teacher Program, A Sixth Year Report.* Trenton, NJ: N.J. State Department of Education.

Odden, Allan, and Sharon Conley. 1991. "Restructuring Teacher Compensation Systems to Foster Collegiality and Help Accomplish National Education Goals." Working Paper No. 2, Center for Research in Education Finance. University of Southern California, September.

Pauly, Edward. 1991. *The Classroom Crucible.* New York: Basic Books.

Perry, Nancy C. 1981. "New Teachers: Do the Best Get Hired?" *Phi Delta Kappan* 63, 2 (October): 113-114.

Pigge, Fred. 1985. "Teacher Education Graduates: Comparisons of Those Who Teach and Do Not Teach," *Journal of Teacher Education* 36, 4 (July-August): 27-28.

Ravitch, Diane. 1995. *National Standards in American Education: A Citizen's Guide.* Washington, DC: Brookings Institution.

Ruenzel, David. 1995. "A Choice in the Matter," *Education Week (*September 27): 23-28.

Schlechty, Phillip C., and Victor S. Vance. 1981. "Do Academically Able Teachers Leave Education? The North Carolina Case," *Phi Delta Kappan* 63, 2 (October): 106-112.

Shavelson, Richard J., et al. 1989. *Indicators for Monitoring Mathematics and Science Education.* Santa Monica, CA: RAND.

Smith, Valerie E., and Julia B. Lee. 1990. "Gender Equity in Teachers' Salaries: A Multilevel Approach," *Educational Evaluation and Policy Analysis,* 12, 1 (Spring): 57-81.

Solmon, Lewis C. 1975. "The Definition of College Quality and Its Impact on Earnings," *Explorations in Economic Research* 2: 537-587.

Sowell, Thomas. 1993. *Inside American Education.* New York: Free Press.

Strauss, Robert P., and Elizabeth A. Sawyer. 1986. "Some New Evidence on Teacher and Student Competencies," *Economics of Education Review* 5, 1: 41-48.

Summers, Anita A., and Barbara L. Wolfe. 1977. "Do Schools Make a Difference?" *American Economic Review* 67, 4 (September): 639-652.

Theobald, Neil. 1990. "An Examination of the Influence of Personal, Professional and School District Characteristics on Public School Teacher Retention," *Economics of Education Review* 9, 3 (Summer): 241-250.

Toch, Thomas. 1991. *In the Name of Excellence.* Oxford: Oxford University Press.

U.S. Department of Education. 1990. *Programs and Plans of the National Center for Education Statistics.* Washington, DC: National Center for Education Statistics.

_____. 1993. *Digest of Educational Statistics.* Washington, DC: National Center for Education Statistics.

Uzell, Lawrence A. 1983. "Where Is the 'Merit' in New Merit-Pay Plans?" Education Week 3, 2 (September 14): 24.

Valente, William O. 1987. *Law in the Schools.* Columbus, OH: Merrill.

Vance, Victor S., and Phillip C. Schlechty. 1982. "The Distribution of Academic Ability in the Teaching Force: Policy Implications," *Phi Delta Kappan* 64, 1 (September): 22-27.

176

Walberg, Herbert J. 1993. "Losing Local Control of Education: Cost and Quality Implications." Reprinted in *Network News and Views*, January. Indianapolis, IN: Educational Excellence Network.

Wayson, William W. 1988. *Up From Excellence: The Impact of the Excellence Movement on Schools*. Bloomington, IN: Phi Delta Kappan Educational Foundation.

Weaver, W. Timothy. 1978. "Educators in Supply and Demand: Effects on Quality," *School Review* 86, 4 (August): 552-93.

_____. 1979. "In Search of Quality: The Need for Talent in Teaching," *Phi Delta Kappan* 61, 1 (September): 29-46.

_____. 1983. *America's Teacher Quality Problem: Alternatives for Reform.* New York: Praeger.

Webster, William J. 1988. "Selecting Effective Teachers," *Journal of Educational Research* 91, 4 (March/April): 245-253.

White, Halbert. 1980. "A Heteroskedasticity-Consistent Covariance Matrix Estimator and a Direct Test for Heteroskedasticity," *Econometrica* 48: 817-838.

Winkler, Donald R. 1975. "Educational Achievement and School Peer Group Composition," *Journal of Human Resources* 10, 3 (Spring): 189-204.

Wise, Arthur E. 1992. "Discussion." In *Teacher Supply, Demand, and Quality*, Erling E. Boe and Dorothy M. Gilford, eds. Washington, DC: National Academy Press.

Wise, Arthur E., et al. 1987. *Effective Teacher Selection: From Recruitment to Retention.* Santa Monica, CA: RAND.

Wolter, Kirk M. 1985. *Introduction to Variance Estimation.* New York: Springer-Verlag.

Wooster, Martin M. 1994. *Angry Classrooms, Vacant Minds.* San Francisco: Pacific Research Institute for Public Policy.

Zarkin, Gary. 1985. "Occupational Choice: An Application to the Market for Public School Teachers," *Quarterly Journal of Economics* 100 (May): 409-446.

INDEX

Academic record
  as basis for teachers compensation,
    13
  as indicator of effective teachers, 9
  significance in teaching and other
    professions, 82
  teacher's record related to student
    learning, 11
Academic standards
  effect of proposed teachers', 116-17
  private schools, 140
  proposed raising of students', 119-21
  state-level, 120
Accountability, proposed school and
  teacher, 120-21
Akerlof, George, 112
*Allen v. Alabama State Board of
  Education*, 118
Alternative Public Schools, Nashville,
  150
Applicants for teaching positions
  criteria for screening, 76-79
  factors influencing quality, 105-6
  model of applicant pool composition,
    83, 95-104
  relation between screening and
    quality, 65-74
  school district screening of, 77-78
Ashford, Brenda G., 108
Attrition, teacher
  effect of salary levels on, 53
  model of relation to demand for
    teachers, 89-91
  related to job availability, 62-64, 89-
    91
  relation to salary levels, 38

Ballou, Dale, 10, 38, 77
Barriers to entry
  under alternative certification
    programs, 113-14
  certification requirements as, 110-13
  for private school teachers, 141

in professions other than teaching, 21
  proposed reforms to lower, 164
Barro, Robert J., 56
Beales, Janet R., 150
Beaudin, Barbara, 12, 84
Benefits
  comparison of public and private
    school, 133-36
  private school in-kind, 154n2
Berlitz Jr., 150
Bishop, John, 106
Bok, Derek, 106
Bonuses, proposed system, 109
Bowles, Samuel, 10
Boyer, Ernest L., 3
Brandt, Richard M., 11, 108
Brewer, Dominic J., 10
Bridges, Edwin M., 122-2
Bryk, Anthony S., 134
Burks, Mary Paxton, 110

California Basic Education Skills Test,
  117
Career path choices
  of college graduates, 65-66
  model of prospective teacher's, 83,
    95-104
Career paths, teacher
  model of duration related to salary,
    62-65
  relation to quality of undergraduate
    institution, 65-66
Carnegie Forum on Education and the
  Economy, 3
Certification
  alternative programs, 113-14
  rates (1976-91), 56-57
  rates for new full-time teachers
    (1990), 61
  recommendations to change methods
    for, 106-7, 110-15
  relation to demand and employment
    opportunity, 56-57, 66, 83

177

178

in professions other than teaching,
81-82
relation to teacher attrition, 62-65,
89-91
of teachers (1976-91), 56-57, 105
teaching in private school, 82
See also Job protection; Tenure

Feistritzer, C. Emily, 113, 114, 115
Ferguson, Ronald F., 10
Finn, Chester E., 151, 153
Frankel, Martin, 45, 54

Galambos, Eva C., 100
Gilford, Dorothy, 63, 77
Goals 2000 curriculum guidelines, 119
Greiner, John M., 108

Haney, Walter, 11,12
Hanushek, Eric, 3, 10, 11, 13, 78, 85,
116
Hatry, Harry P., 108
Hoffer, Thomas, 140
Holmes Group, The, 3, 116
Hood, Stafford, 118
Huntington Learning Centers, 150
Hutton, Jerry B., 113

Incentives, performance-based
career ladder, 127n2
efforts to initiate, 55
public and private schools, 137-40
teaching and other professions, 81-82
Institutions, undergraduate
attended by private school teachers,
130
private school teachers from quality,
142-43
quality related to graduates' career
paths, 65-66
relation between quality, pay, and
working conditions, 68-69
relation to teachers' salaries and
workforce quality, 24-29
See also Schools of education

Interdistrict school choice, 149
Internship programs, 54, 115, 145
Iowa Tests of Basic Skills, 10
Iowa Tests of Educational
Development, 10

Jacobson, Stephen L., 31
James, Estelle, 10, 99
Job opportunities. *See* Employment
opportunities
Job protection
with certification, 112-13
under Massachusetts education
reform (1993), 123
Massachusetts Education Reform Act
(1993), 123
for tenured teachers, 122-23

Kelley, Carolyn, 12
Kirst, Michael W., 12
Koerner, James D., 1

Labor force, teacher. *See* Workforce,
teacher model of relation between
turnover and quality of, 77-79, 93-94
Labor market
applicants from selective colleges in,
66-670
for professions other than teaching,
81-82
in undesirable locations, 31-34
See also Employment opportunities;
Recruitment, teacher
Labor market for teachers
barriers to entry, 110-11
demand, 61-65, 83, 89-91
entry-level positions, 55-56
excess supply in, 56-58, 75
features of, 53
flow of newly certified teachers
(1976-91), 56-57
impact of structural features, 163
supply, 56-62
See also Barriers to entry
Lankford, Hamilton, 31

Programs of study
  leading to teaching certification, 54
Public schools. *See* Schools, public

Quality, labor force
  model of teacher turnover and, 93-94

Ravitch, Diane, 9, 120
Recruitment, teacher
  impediments to hiring better teachers,
    164
  incentives other than salary, 39
  influence of teacher attributes on, 70-
    74
  of new teachers, 31-34
  by private schools, 140-41
  problems of, 2
  public schools, 140
  quality of new recruits (1980s), 16-21
  recommendations to change patterns
    of, 106-7
  relation to state-level salary increases,
    21-36
  in undesirable locations, 31
Rees, Daniel, 53
Rudner, Lawrence, 55, 117

Salaries, teacher
  debate over, 3-5
  impact of higher, 8-9, 12, 24-29, 49-
    50, 163
  increases (1979-1989), 4, 7, 21, 105
  levels (1976-91), 56
  link to employment opportunity, 62,
    107
  of private school teachers, 111
  private sector flexibility of, 139, 141
  proposed differentiation on basis of
    merit, 107-9
  of public and private sector, 130
  recommended raising of, 3-4, 13, 15,
    106
  regressions on public and private
    school, 157-62

relation to principals' ratings, 34-36,
  51-52
relation to prospective education
  majors' SAT scores, 21-24
relative by state (1979), 21-22
in salary schedules, 55
state-level increases and workforce
  quality, 24-29, 49-50
of teacher-mentors in California,
  156n12
See also Merit pay plans
Salary schedules
  private schools, 137
  for public-school teacher
    compensation, 55, 137
SAT scores
  education majors and prospective
    education majors, 1-2, 11-12, 16
  relation between salary changes and
    (1979-89), 21-23
Sawyer, Elizabeth A., 11
Schlechty, Phillip C., 18, 77
School boards, local
  control over charter schools, 153
  in debate over salaries, 4-5
School choice
  criticism of plans, 149, 151-52
  interdistrict choice, 149
  limitations of plans, 151
  magnet schools, 149
  vouchers, 149
Schools, charter
  Arizona, 152-53
  criticism of and opposition to, 148-
    49, 153
  experimental school choice plan, 149
  noncertified teachers in, 114
  populations served, 151
  regulation of and restrictions on, 153
Schools, magnet, 149
Schools, private
  claim of better education in, 129
  comparison of teachers in public and,
    130-33

184

About the Institute

The W.E. Upjohn Institute for Employment Research is a nonprofit research organization devoted to finding and promoting solutions to employment-related problems at the national, state, and local level. It is an activity of the W.E. Upjohn Unemployment Trustee Corporation, which was established in 1932 to administer a fund set aside by the late Dr. W.E. Upjohn, founder of The Upjohn Company, to seek ways to counteract the loss of employment income during economic downturns.

The Institute is funded largely by income from the W.E. Upjohn Unemployment Trust, supplemented by outside grants, contracts, and sales of publications. Activities of the Institute are comprised of the following elements: (1) a research program conducted by a resident staff of professional social scientists; (2) a competitive grant program, which expands and complements the internal research program by providing financial support to researchers outside the Institute; (3) a publications program, which provides the major vehicle for the dissemination of research by staff and grantees, as well as other selected work in the field; and (4) an Employment Management Services division, which manages most of the publicly funded employment and training programs in the local area.

The broad objectives of the Institute's research, grant, and publication programs are to: (1) promote scholarship and experimentation on issues of public and private employment and unemployment policy; and (2) make knowledge and scholarship relevant and useful to policymakers in their pursuit of solutions to employment and unemployment problems.

Current areas of concentration for these programs include: causes, consequences, and measures to alleviate unemployment; social insurance and income maintenance programs; compensation; workforce quality; work arrangements; family labor issues; labor-management relations; and regional economic development and local labor markets.